The Conservative Manifesto

William T. Hennessy

Right Press, Inc.
Groton, Connecticut

The author gratefully acknowledges the cooperation of many publishers in obtaining permission to use their materials in this book.

Copyright (c) 1993 by William T. Hennessy

All rights reserved. No part of this book may be reproduced in any form or by any electronic or mechanical means, including information storage and retrieval systems without permission in writing from the publisher, except by a reviewer, who may quote brief passages in review.

Printed in the United States of America.

First Edition.

Library of Congress Cataloging-in-Publication Data
Hennessy, William T.
  The Conservative Manifesto/by William T. Hennessy
  "A Right Press book."

  ISBN 0-9638816-0-4

  1. United States-Politics and Government-Political Science. 2. Politics, Practical-United States-Political Science.

Library of Congress number 93-093642

Right Press, Inc.
5 Magnolia Drive
Groton, CT 06340

First Printing.

To Patrick J. Mahon,
my uncle,
mentor,
tutor,
and inspiration.

Contents

Acknowledgments

Forward   7

Chapter One   *The War's Origins*   11

Chapter Two   *The Current Conditions*   17

Chapter Three   *The Conservative Creed*   38

Chapter Four   *Liberal vs. Conservative Defined*   43

Chapter Five   *Conservative Milestones*   49

Chapter Six   *Beginning Steps*   69

Chapter Seven   *Fighting the War for the Soul of America*   76

Chapter Eight   *Summary and Conclusions*   93

Appendix   *The American Ideal*   97

Bibliography   *103*

Acknowledgements

Sitting at a borrowed computer, thinking back over the 29 years of my life, trying to figure out who to thank and who to ignore for my having finally completed my first book, I fear these acknowledgements may grow to be longer than any chapter, so full is my life with wonderful people.

First and foremost I must thank my wife, Julie, who performed like a shepherd keeping our four children, Amie, Jack, Benjamin, and Patrick, away from me for hours upon hours. She changed diapers, cooked dinner, washed dishes, folded laundry, took the children to swimming lessons, took the children to the store, went grocery shopping, vacuumed the house, washed the car, stripped and refinished an antique armoire, brought me beers, brought me cigarettes, delivered mail, chased Benjamin (2 years) down the street, and all of these on a daily basis. She encouraged and supported my writing when editors all across the fruited plain said I'd make a great veterinarian. She is at least half responsible for this book.

Next, of course, Mom and Dad, who worked hideous hours in unglamorous jobs to give me a first rate Catholic school education, kindergarten through high school graduation and on into college. They also instilled in me the American ideal of individual achievement which is at the heart of this book. They never gave up on me when they had every opportunity (and probably the strong desire) to do so. Each of God's children deserve them as parents.

My Uncle Patrick J. Mahon is the wisest and perhaps most learned man I have ever met. He sacrifices to this day for everyone but himself. He worked beyond the limits of child labor laws to feed his family during the depression. He fought in World War II. He's read virtually every book worth reading, memorized every important civil war battle and personality, and raised a family. He has been my mentor, but much more. Without him, this book could not have been written.

My Aunt Mame Mahon guided, directed, and encouraged me as only a friend can. She gave advice that brought me into adulthood ready to fight the good fight. She kept much of the family's history that would inspire me when I needed help.

My sisters, Mary, Sue, and Mickey, made it through the miserable 1960s and 1970s intact. For that they deserve great credit. As the youngest and only boy of four children, I was spoiled rotten and they were my spoilers. But there is nothing wrong with being spoiled, so long as you are the spoiled one and not the victim of the spoiled one, so I thank them.

Jeffery Fellows forced me off my laurels. He made me start a company. He made me write this book. He proofed and edited it professionally. He invested in my work's success. He deserves all the credit for this book which is left over after my family has taken its share.

Eric and Barbara Cohen proofed, edited, and encouraged. I thank them for their time, efforts, and outstanding suggestions. The people who developed WordPerfect word processing software gave me what no one else could: spell check. Thanks to them. Sr. Barbara Schlatter, O.P., teaches English at Bishop DuBourg High School in St. Louis. I took away more good writing skills than I ever let on in my composition assignments. Others responsible for this book include Darrell Schwoch at Network Printers in Milwaukee, WI, for outstanding printing services, Dave and Greg Miller at Milprin in Groton, CT, who do all my local printing, Mr. Ted Nichols for his book *How To Publish a Book and Sell a Million Copies*, the late E.B. White and William Strunk Jr. for their separate efforts on *The Elements of Style*.

Finally, I must thank William F. Buckley Jr. and Patrick J. Buchanan whose columns in the St. Louis Globe-Democrat from 1975 until I joined the Navy in 1984 made me think and write the way I do. To Mr. Buckley goes my special thanks for carrying the conservative banner consistently and brilliantly for a lifetime. He deserves thanks from all quarters.

W. T. Hennessy, Aug. 14, 1993
Groton, Connecticut

Forward

Alarm is in order over the condition of America. This conclusion comes from looking back to a starting point in what Pat Buchanan has called the war for the soul of America, and tracing its development to the present day. This war for our country's soul is the same war that William F. Buckley Jr. described as a battle between Good and Evil, between God and Satan, between individualism and collectivism, capitalism and communism -- more than three decades ago. In 1993 America, it is known as the war between conservatism and liberalism.

During the Great Depression liberalism surrendered its romantic mantle, becoming pro-socialist, Soviet apologists taking over the bureaus and agencies of government, and usurping extra-Constitutional powers from the people for the benefit of the state. Under the protection of moral relativism and Keynesian economics, these liberals changed the American government from the limited, peace-keeping union of states envisioned by the founders into an enormous and sprawling power vessel. This changed the relationship of the individual to his government and was the first shot in this war.

Conservatism's first retaliation came as a horizontal salvo fired almost simultaneously by conservative leaders William F. Buckley Jr., with *Up From Liberalism* in 1959, and Senator Barry Goldwater, with *The Conscience of a Conservative* in 1960. While conservatism predates these books (Buckley, alone, had already founded *National Review* magazine and written three books), no national conservative movement that challenged liberalism for power existed until these two books stirred people's souls. The war for the soul of America, then, began in earnest in 1960.

My concern comes from looking back to those two books and assessing what has happened since. My conclusion: If the war ends today, or in the near future, conservatives lose.

Item   In *The Conscience of a Conservative*, Barry Goldwater lamented that welfare spending represented the second largest appropriation in the federal government, second only to defense.[1]

Item   In *Up From Liberalism*, Buckley declared, "I will not cede more power to the state. I will not willingly cede more power to anyone, not to the state, not to General Motors, not to the CIO. I will hoard my power like a miser, resisting every effort to drain it away from me. I will then use *my* power as *I* see fit."[2]

---

[1] Barry Goldwater, The Conscience of a Conservative (New York: Victor Publishing Co., 1960) Reprinted for Campus Books, 1973.

[2] William F. Buckley Jr., Up From Liberalism (New York: Stein and Day, first paperback edition, 1985).

Judging the score by these boldest volleys of our first battle, we are losing. Defense spending in fiscal year 1994 will be far less than social spending, and in ensuing years will represent a continually smaller portion of the federal budget. Mr. Buckley, despite his Herculean efforts to resist, has ceded much more power to the state -- more between 1960 and today than in his previous thirty-five years.

This governmental usurpation of power coupled with liberalism's "all things are relative" moral philosophy has created a void in the soul of America which is filling up with the foulest sewage of human moral decay. We celebrate whores and sodomites for their public, prideful reveling in sin and decadence. The leading personas of our culture worship the *in utero* mutilation and murder of babies, to the score of 1.6 million a year. Amidst economic stagnation, our taxes increase constantly to fund condom distribution to fifth graders, welfare abortions, and socialist redistribution plans. Some might ask, "Is *this America*, then, worth trying to save?"

The conservative answer must be, "Yes."

Therefore, critics and liberals and sensitive "progressive" conservatives be damned. I will fight for the America Frank Capra depicted in his movies. I will fight for the America whose streets were lined with gold in the imaginations of immigrants. I will fight for an America where children retain their childhoods. I begin my fight on these pages. If you disagree with some of my observations, we will work it out. If, however, the very idea of this book offends you, you are the enemy.

> "And 'mid the tumult Kubla heard from far
> Ancestral voices prophesying war."
> -S.T. Coleridge, *Kubla Khan*

The War's Origins

Today's America is not the America to which our birth rights entitled us. Our America is a quasi-socialist cesspool of political intolerance, class hatred, bureaucratic micromanagement, and cultural stench. Liberal control of America's culture centers transformed our society into something more like Ted Kennedy's America than like Harry Truman's. We are a people subject to virtual ownership by the political and academic classes which disdain ordinary as worthless, common as unenlightened, and traditional as atavistic. Among our present administration's leaders, the very words "ordinary," "common," and "traditional" represent the vices against which they resolved to fight when they entered upon their public and professional lives -- evils which must be exposed and destroyed.

Some prominent conservatives today espouse far more optimism than is due. They see the 1990s and Bill Clinton's attacks on tradition as brief throwbacks to the 1960s and 1970s, when such ideas as sexual liberation, gender- and race-based rights, atheism, statism, and radicalism were in vogue. They believe that the 1980s, and particularly the Reagan years, represented the actual state of American culture, and that after its brief flirtation with liberalism, the country will fall right back into traditional ranks and march in its conservative step. They seem to believe that this conservative resurrection will come about automatically, like a season of the year. But the rebirth of the American ideal is far too important and noble a cause to leave to the whim of nature, even human nature. Conservatism *is on the verge of victory*, but we stand on the precipe of that victory still, unmoving, unmoved. As we wait, liberalism advances further, the individual loses more power, the war for the soul of America becomes more difficult. To win, we must first be moved to fight. Before we fight, we must arm.

Even more dangerous to our heritage than conservative complacency, however, is the pseudo-conservative's misguided interpretation of public attitudes. The lessons to be learned from the 1980s were that a) Supply Side Economics works, b) Americans want their fellow-citizens to behave in compliance with Judeo-Christian tradition regardless of personal beliefs, c) the sharper the contrast between the conservative and the liberal the bigger the conservative victory, and d) America is predominantly conservative in nature. Some in the Republican party who claim to be conservatives are actually, like Bill Clinton, devoid of an ideological base. They think conservatives lost ground in elections between 1986 and 1992 by being too conservative. In fact, the opposite is true.

Time has come for both the complacent and pseudo-conservatives to wake up and take the lead in the fight against the liberal erosion of Western Civilization, or GET OUT OF OUR WAY! Why?

The majority of Americans may reason and behave as conservatives, may wish Reagan were still President, may hope the 1980s repeat themselves, but the real power in America remains in liberal hands.

Liberals began their march to conquer American culture in the 1920s, at the beginning of what Paul Johnson calls "modern times"[1]. They started in academia, spreading during the New Deal, to the labor movement and government, devouring the popular media, infiltrating the churches, and changing the course of political debate. Seizing final power in the 1960s, these invaders from the left subverted the peace, civil rights, and women's movements. By the time of Ronald Reagan's election, liberals owned the fountains of thought and the time clocks of scholarly debate: the dominant media, the editorial staffs of most major newspapers and magazines, the board rooms of corporations, major elements of the armed forces, all of the federal government, most of the state governments, all of the labor unions, all of Hollywood, all of Broadway, all of the major book publishing companies, most of the social sciences, all of literature, and nearly all of public school education. Liberalism had, by 1978, achieved all of its strategic objectives save for the last and most important: Eliminating the individual as a political unit.

The survival of the individual, at least in spirit, provided Reagan's victories, and influenced the policies and attitudes

---

[1] Modern Times: The World from the Twenties to the Eighties, (New York: HarperCollins, 1984). Copyright (c) 1983 by Paul Johnson.

that dominated the surface of American life during Reagan's tenure. Whatever retreats were made during the 1980s, however, were made by those very same conservatives who seemed in charge. The liberal march did not stop on January 20, 1981; it traded its combat boots for sneakers. The battle to subordinate the individual to the state went on, but in the periphery, in the shadows, where the cold, remorseless light of day could not touch it. Conservatism, like talk of a return to traditional American values, only skimmed the surface.

Conservatives have practiced a sort of political denial since the early 1980s. We've spent thirteen years denying liberalism's strangle hold on our culture, just as some cancer victims avoid the doctor, for fear of recognizing and having to come to grips with the disease. But liberalism was never in remission. Like a tumor, it grew deeper roots and a solid trunk during the Reagan era only to sprout its collectivist leaves from rejuvenated and new branches in the springtime of Clinton, taking conservatives by surprise.

And most conservatives fail to respond to the symptoms even today. From what we are told is the political right we hear dangerous talk about "moving to the center" "celebrating diversity," and "building a big tent." These are pseudo-conservative euphemisms for "acting like liberals," "talking like liberals," and "appeasing liberals" -- dangerous symptoms of continued denial. The conservative tent should be open to all who wish to become conservatives, but should be heavily fortified against liberals in Reagan's clothing who seek to make conservatism fit *them* instead of *reforming themselves* into conservatives.

With victory in sight, our demise is equally near. The tumor continues to grow, now fertilized by the executive branch. Authentic conservatives must force the optimistic, tame, quiet, armchair conservative's unwilling finger onto the telltale lump, take him to the physician for a final diagnosis, force him to face the reality of the liberal disease within, and attack the tumor of liberalism with a phalanx of treatments that will kill either the disease or the patient. The prescription may seem desperate, cruel, but it has become necessary. If begun soon enough and prosecuted zealously, my prescription will prove effective.

Success in our quest to replace the welfare, collectivist, morally relative state with the American ideal[2] requires a strong argument, both from me to you and from you to the world at large. I will set the course for action by a) briefly reviewing the current conditions (as if anyone needs reminding about how screwed up this country is), b) offering a conservative creed to guide our interpretations of policies, events, and directions, c) defining the differences between liberalism and conservatism, d) offering several major policy objectives which, when enacted, will serve both to measure the progress of our war and to reverse the current socialistic, atheistic trends in America, e) providing a list of resources for the soldier in the battle and f) giving specific directions on how we should conduct the war.

My argument is not the only one that can be made for conservatism, nor is it necessarily the best. The highest

---

[2] For a detailed examination of the American ideal, see appendix I of this book.

hope I have for this book is that it will reinvigorate the conservative movement started by Buckley and Goldwater and which reached its peak with the election of Ronald Reagan. My argument is meant for the rank-and-file conservative, the Reagan Democrats, the men and women who know, instinctively, that something is wrong with their country. It is also for the young men and women who, reaching the age of reason, are fed platitudes of feeling instead of logic and truth. They need direction which, if their minds are truly open, this book may provide.

In *Up From Liberalism*[3], William F. Buckley Jr. admitted that, "There is no conservative political manifesto which, as we make our faltering way, we can consult, confident that it will point a sure finger in the direction of the good society." When Mr. Buckley gave us fair warning in 1959, many conservatives failed to take heed and respond. Now, thirty-four years later, many opportunities are past. The choice for America today is to fight for the return of Western Civilization in our society, government, and culture, or accept the liberal Eastern barbarism that sits patiently waiting, like a vulture, to feed on the carcass of American individualism.

Let this be that manifesto which starts the war.

---

[3] ibid.

"It would seem that, if despotism were to be established among the democratic nations of our days, it might assume a different character; it would be more extensive and more mild; it would degrade men without tormenting them."[4]
 -Alexis de Tocqueville, *Democracy in America*

The Current Conditions

Just tuning into the evening news ought to convince everyone that action is needed, but perhaps conservatives require a stronger jolt to get moving. Maybe the dominant media culture has lulled even the right into thinking Bill Clinton, if given a chance and given his way, can save America. But he cannot, would not fix our problems. What we see as America's problems, liberals see as America's selling features. Let's evaluate where America stands.

Your country, my country, our children's country may have already deteriorated beyond hope. The federal government controls virtually every private decision in our lives through a spider web network of bureaus and agencies built rock-solid during the New Deal and reinforced,

---

[4] For a fuller examination of Tocqueville's image of despotism in democratic times, see <u>Democracy in America</u>, Part II, Book four.

refinanced, and rearmed ever since. This bureaucracy network feeds off political and economic power usurped from the people. The despotism Tocqueville predicted 153 years ago has come to pass.

The bureaucracy network regenerates with each college graduation ceremony and, thus, has become self-perpetuating. It is owned and operated by America's far left: the National Organization for Women, the Rainbow Coalition, the Sierra Club, Earth First, Greenpeace, People for the American Way, Americans for Democratic Action, ACT-UP, Queer Nation, the Gay and Lesbian Task Force, and the rest of the anti-capitalist, anti-morality hit squads. Congress, the major media, the labor unions, and Hollywood are wholly-owned subsidiaries of this leviathan beast. You, the individual, are *nothing to the bureaucracy* but a feeding pod to be sucked dry in its unquenchable thirst for power.

Meanwhile, our citizenry has become, to a large extent, a day-care center of litigation-crazed cry babies who want Uncle Government to make life completely risk-free by distributing happiness in a pill free of charge. Author Charles J. Sykes recently described the American of the 1990s quite accurately: "Americans expect life to be painfree [sic]. A disease is something that happens to you, not something you're responsible for . . . if you sleep around, gamble away your money, drink yourself into the gutter, or ignore your family, you are no longer irresponsible but merely in need of treatment."

This image of the modern American is not only accurate, it is and ought to be frightening. Risk is what one accepts in exchange for the opportunity to achieve happiness. Without risk, there is no happiness, though Americans today seem to believe the reverse. Our citizens think that happiness, like health care, retirement planning, and a college education, is an entitlement owed to them by their government. As Sykes said, the only cure for our phobias of risk and pain is a return to a shared moral language where character and actions define the person, rather than the degree of victimization and membership in some phoney oppressed group.[5]

As I hinted earlier, conservatives prefer reaction over activism. Before we forsake the safety and comfort of the sofa for the weapons of a soldier in the culture war, something or someone must convince us of the need for immediate and massive mobilization. Three aspects of civilization which touch every person in America have, over the past 40 years, touched us exclusively in the wrong way. The best titles for these three areas are The Economic Sewer System, The Social Septic Tank, and The Cultural Waste Dump.

The Economic Sewer System. Freedom from confiscatory taxes that went to pay for things the people didn't want was one of the top reasons given for

---

[5] Elizabeth Weise, AP, in <u>The Day of New London</u>, August 13, 1993.

immigrating to America in the years 1815 to 1830.[6] Clearly, things have changed for the worse.

In 1920, the federal government consumed just three percent of the Gross National Product. Combined with state and local taxes, twenty percent of GNP went to pay for government. In 1993, it takes more than 40 cents of every dollar earned to pay for our national, state, and local governance. Unfortunately, most of these taxes fund programs which benefit few of the people who pay the taxes. Liberals call this fairness. Economists call it stagnation. This stifling taxation has bought a pile of government junk we never asked for, have no idea what to do with, and cannot afford.

As everyone heard until blue in the face during the 1992 presidential campaign, the American standard of living doubled every other generation from the 1920s through the 1950s, but now the standard of living can be expected to double only every 120 years. (In reality, the standard of living will not double in 120 years, or a million and twenty years, if we continue on our present path. But more on that in due course.)

This year's economic growth, the increase in Gross Domestic Product (GDP) over last year's, will be something around two percent. Last year's GDP growth was about the same. It was a little slower in 1991 and slightly higher in 1990. 1989 was no banner year. These

---

[6] Paul Johnson, <u>The Birth of the Modern</u>, (New York: HarperCollins, 1991). Copyright (c) 1991 by Paul Johnson.

five years will go down among the slowest five year period for our economy this century. Unemployment, thought licked for good during the 1980s, has increased steadily since 1990 to about seven percent. Additionally, many jobs are part-time or low wage service positions which do not provide a significant amount of left over cash for savings (investment) and spending (which creates more jobs). The marginal propensity to consume is high among five dollar an hour workers who get a 50 cent an hour raise, but when compared to the whole economy ($3 trillion) such increases are virtually meaningless. Further, these increases go almost exclusively for more or better necessities rather than new, different items, thus concentrating new spending into limited areas of food, energy, and clothing. Savings is not even a consideration for low wage earners, because other things are needed.

Large corporations are continually, it seems, cutting payrolls rather than increasing them. Daily news reports bring stories of another two or three major employers laying off more employees. Small business are not hiring because 1) people are not buying, 2) too much uncertainty exists regarding tax increases, 3) too much uncertainty over mandated health care provision costs, 4) too much uncertainty over new regulations, and 5) the cost of employment is too high because of government mandated benefits.

You can skip CNBC's business reports, forget CNN's money and throw away *The Wall Street Journal*, *Investor's Business Daily*, and your *Kiplinger's Newsletter*. I can tell you what the economy will do for the next three years: absolutely nothing.

The current feeling in the White House, the left side of Congress, and even many of the Fortune 500 board rooms is that we need more government regulations, higher taxes, more social spending, more mandated benefits, and more government "investment" in really fancy companies that make really fancy gadgets.

I started discussion of the economy by paraphrasing Paul Johnson's explanation of why many people left Europe for America and other places at the start of the last century. But before 1815, history tells us, people were leaving Europe for approximately the same reasons; they didn't like the way European governments functioned. America was founded as a rejection of the European ways. Paul Johnson provides a sense of what it was like to get away from European taxation to an America with "No poor rates [taxes], because virtually no poor. An American farm which kept eight horses paid only $12 annually in tax. To Europeans such figures were incredible. Not only were American wage rates high, but you kept what you received."[7]

Alexis de Tocqueville noticed a sharp contrast between America and Europe when he visited here in 1838. "Nothing is more striking to a European traveller in the United States," he wrote, "than the absence of what we term the Government, or the Administration . . . [In

---

[7] ibid.

America, t]he hand which moves the social machine is invisible."[8]

Do today's European visitors notice the differences that Johnson's visitor and Tocqueville noticed? I doubt it.

Today we have forgotten all about that American economic ideal. We hear that we should become more like Europe, even from some conservatives who talk about a "right" to free health care, a "right" to the family and emergency leave bill, a "right" to a minimum wage, a "right" to social security, a "right" to quotas. Such conservatives stand abreast their liberal colleagues, point toward the Atlantic ocean, and extol the "wonderful systems in Germany, Norway, Sweden, and Denmark." Then they point north to Canada and cheer its government as it raises taxes to finance more socialism.

Those who support importing European-style socialism are either liars or fools. They may tell us that European and Canadian socialism works, but it provably does not. In England nearly half of the people covered by mandated, "free" medicine buy private health insurance out of their own pocket -- better than dying in line at one of the government hospitals or clinics, they reason. In Buffalo, New York, hospitals have to reserve Saturdays for their Canadian patients who pay cash for services which no amount of money can buy from Canada's socialist health care programs. In fact, there are more magnetic resonance

---

[8] Alexis de Tocqueville, <u>Democracy in America</u> (New York: Mentor Books, 1984) Copyright (c) by Richard D. Heffner, editor.

imagery machines in the city of Philadelphia than in all of Canada, and Canadian doctors are fleeing their homeland for, what is comparatively, the practitioner's paradise: America.

Thanks to socialism, European unemployment is above ten percent, as is Canada's. Young Germans looking for work are so happy with their government's socialist programs that some have taken to murdering foreigners believed to be stealing jobs. In fact, not foreigners, but governments all across Europe steal jobs through the misguided, moron economics that many want us to adopt. Socialist governments seize capital from good, productive, private businesses with which to create layers and layers of low-wage bureaucracy jobs that contribute absolutely nothing to the economy, the culture, or the society.

And some in this country want to build a similar, failed system here. Democrats, the party in power, the party we elected to power, the party that has controlled the House of Representatives for 40 consecutive years (11 years before I was born), want more unemployment in America, less health care at higher prices, weaker businesses, slower growth, more class hatred, more welfare queens, fewer business start ups, less entrepreneurial drive, and less achievement. They will lie, saying they want no such things. But the historically undeniable results of the programs they advocate prove otherwise. As these negative economic consequences mount, more people become dependent on the gracious handouts of government. These government dependents -- slaves, if you will -- are called "constituents" in the parlance of Washington. Unlike the old fashioned thinking, remembering, and voting constituents, though, these enslaved constituents cannot vote their masters out of office. Without Master Government feeding them, they will starve! "And you vote out Uncle Rostie, well, who's gonna shovel money at you then?"

That's how the economic sewer system works. Money comes out of the private economy, through taxes and regulation, and into the Washington economy. The Washington economy is a closed loop: If you don't work for the government, you may not participate, unless, of course, you'd like to become a slave to government. As more and more money leaves the real economy for Washington's, fewer and fewer companies have enough money left to hire new employees. Since our government isn't kind enough to shoot these left-over employees and put them out of their misery, it admits them into the Washington economy -- as slaves. (By the way, no emancipation legislation is currently pending on Capitol Hill.)

The federal government's payroll is larger than any company's in America. It is larger than any two companies'. And it grows larger every day. As the federal payroll increases, the rate of private economic growth diminishes. Through direct taxation and the indirect taxation of regulation (mandatory health care, mandatory retirement plans, mandatory time off for child care, mandatory hiring quotas) the government siphons off as much as 45% of the country's capacity to produce. In other words, if the federal government went on hiatus January 1, 1994 for one year, next year's GDP growth could be 45%.

How many jobs would expansion of this magnitude create? God only knows.

But mere mortals may understand this: until we not only break the growth of government, but shrink government in real size, 3% GDP growth will seem like a windfall.

The Social Septic Tank. Ask which social problems are most damaging to America today, and the answers may be crime, teenage pregnancy, and poverty. Ask how to fix them, and the answers, according to the popular media, are treat criminals better, teach school children the right way to fornicate, and spend more on welfare programs. Our society seems to believe that punishing criminals causes crime, innocence of things carnal causes teenage pregnancy, and paying people to be poor cures poverty. The American ideal is obviously very faint in America today. These answers demonstrate the classic liberal mind set and prove that liberals control the agenda of social policy in America.

In fact, America has sunk into this sociological abyss because liberals enjoy a 40 year monopoly of social policy.[9] The social policy debate in a healthy America would concentrate on such questions as: **Should** we provide compulsory retirement savings through Social Security? **Should** we provide federal aid to families with dependent children? **Should** we give vouchers for free milk, cereal,

---

[9] This 40 year liberal domination of social policy, not coincidentally, parallels the period that Democrats have controlled the United States House of Representatives.

and formula to pregnant women and new mothers? **Should** we have a Department of Health and Human Services? **Should** we have a Department of Housing and Urban Development? **Should** we have a Department of Education? Today these issues are debated not as "should we?" but as "how much should we?" But merely identifying the merits of dissolving Social Security, AFDC, WIC, HUD, HHS, and Education is grounds for accusations of racism, elitism, and insensitivity from today's hypersensitive Thought Police. No one in public office, even our supposed conservative stalwarts, ever mentions elimination of these counterproductive programs, all of which increase the magnitude of the problems they are intended to solve.

When the government gets involved in any problem, the problem gets worse. For examples, look at two socio-economic problems the government has tried to fix: Poverty and Agriculture.

The first permanent programs designed to end poverty came under the heading "The Great Society," and can be attributed, for sake of simplicity, to Lyndon B. Johnson. These programs, though not necessarily new in the 1960s, were designed to instill a permanent welfare state in America, as distinguished from the programs under Roosevelt and Truman which were designed to be temporary.

Very simply, the result of our war on poverty, 1965 to 1990, is that the number of children living in poverty quadrupled. Thirty million Americans earn less than 60% of the poverty line. Meanwhile, by sociologist Charles Murray's calculations, over 3 trillion dollars have been spent on this war[10], enough, if given directly in cash, to make every poor man, woman, and child one of the rich who Bill Clinton wants to soak. Had we done that, we would have ended poverty for a few years. Instead, we forced the poor to accept the loving, tender, inept, stupid, fumbling, five-thumbed hand of government in the forms of Aid to Families with Dependent Children, Food Stamps, Medicare, Medicaid, Housing and Urban Development, and so on and so forth. Rather than helping the poor, we made poverty a growth industry, and one of the fastest growing growth industries in the free world.

Our first national experiment in solving the problems of farmers began with Franklin Roosevelt. Placing farmers on a pedestal, he determined that, unlike the rest of us, farmers must be exempt from the whims of the market place, so that farming is profitable regardless of the real price consumers are willing to pay for food. This ranks as one of the most absurd and costly brain lapses in history.

The amount of money we have plowed under on America's farms since 1935 is somewhere in the neighborhood of one trillion dollars. That's a fortune to you and me. What that money bought is a national debt of $4 trillion, impoverished farmers, and the best fed enemies in history. With that money, our government bought food at double the market price and gave it to the Soviets so they could spend their money on bigger and more accurate

---

[10] <u>Losing Ground: American Social Policy 1950-1980</u> (New York: Basic Books, 1984). Copyright (c) 1984 by Charles Murray.

missiles aimed at the American farms the government was paying to grow nothing. This is called Farm Price Supports. If you think paying $2.00 for a $.12 loaf of bread is a good idea, the program works.

What the government failed to acknowledge, and continues to ignore, is that America has too damn many farmers growing too much food for too small a market. Farm loans (at 5% even when the rest of us mortals were paying 21% to borrow money for groceries), price supports, and the myriad other agriculture programs Uncle Sam has stuck us with a bill for, have kept millions of people in the farming industry when economic conditions brought about through technological advances demanded that they find another line of work.

The government is 0 for 2, and we haven't even warmed up. Ask yourself this: If you had the money, where would you go to get a haircut? The nearest Army base with government barbers? Or the nearest civilian barber, who starves to death if he gives bad cuts? Now, why would you ever consider going to the government for anything more important? If they can't cut hair, they sure as hell can't grow corn or perform a good bypass operation.

Despite these failures of liberalism, liberals tell us that if we oppose their social programs, we are greedy, selfish, unpatriotic, racist, sexist, homophobic bigots who care nothing for our fellow human and likely pick our noses without the vail of a handkerchief.

One useful tool in demonstrating the decline of the quality of life in America is William J. Bennett's "Index of Leading Cultural Indicators" compiled from various sources in conjunction with Empower America, The Heritage Foundation, and Free Congress Foundation.[11]

From Mr. Bennett we learn the following:

1. Acts of violent crime have increased from 288,460 in 1960 to 1,911,770 by 1991 or 500 percent, while our population increased only 41 percent (FBI). (One may conjecture that had it not been for the rampant violent crime, the population would have increased by a greater degree.) Meanwhile, median prison sentences have *decreased* from 22.5 days in 1954 to 8.0 days by 1990 (National Center for Policy Analysis, 1992). Liberalism seems to be responsible, because both of these statistics *improved during most of Ronald Reagan's administration*.

2. Juvenile violent crime has increased from 137 acts per 100,000 in 1960 to 430.6 per 100,000 in 1990 (FBI, 1991). This statistic's only period of improvement was 1980 to 1986, during Ronald Reagan's presidency.

3. The number of Children on Aid to Families with Dependent Children has increased from 3.5 percent of children in 1960 to 12.9 percent in 1991, again with *decreases during the Reagan years* (U.S. Bureau of the Census; U.S. House of Representatives, 1993).

4. Teen pregnancies (ending in birth or abortion) from 1972 (the year before Roe vs. Wade) through 1990 increased from 49.4 per thousand (5%) to 99.2 per thousand (10%), a 100 percent increase in the teen

---

[11] The Index of Leading Culture Indicators is available from The Heritage Foundation, 214 Massachusetts Ave., N.E., Washington, DC 20002-4999, (202) 546-4400.

pregnancy rate. Abortion among teenagers increased in the same period from 19.9 per thousand pregnancies (2.0%) to 43.8 per thousand pregnancies (4.4%). Assuming that increased teenage sexual activity is, in some measure, increased by the availability of *abortion on demand*, abortion has *increased the number of live births to teenagers*, rather than decreasing the number, as liberals claim abortion will do.

5. Other significantly bad changes in behavior:

- Births to unmarried women: 224,300 in 1960
  1,165,384 in 1990

- Total abortions: 586,800 in 1972
  1,680,000 in 1990

- Child abuse: 669,000 cases in 1976
  2,694,000 cases in 1991

- Teen Suicide Rate: 3.6 per 100,000 in 1960
  11.3 per 100,000 in 1990

- Single Parent Families: 9.1% of families 1960
  28.6% of families 1991

- Average SAT Scores: 975 in 1960
  899 in 1992*

- Daily TV Viewing: 5.06 hours per day 1960
  7.04 hours per day 1992*

(* indicates trend improved during the Reagan years.)

Several important conclusions can be drawn from these data. First, as federal social spending has increased (1960 to 1990), the problems which that spending was purported to solve became worse instead of better. Second, while Ronald Reagan was President, and the rate of increase in social spending was sharply curtailed, the attendant problems subsided concurrently with Reagan's conservative attacks on the problems. Third, when Reagan's years ended and George Bush moved the Presidency away from Reagan's strong conservative principles, the problems began to increase in intensity again.

Drawing the lines out, we can safely predict that under liberal administrations assisted by liberal Congresses, the negative trend lines will turn up sharply as social spending increases. And social spending will increase for at least the next three years.

In addition to the correlation between social spending and social problems, there is a correlation between permissiveness and social problems. Comparing the numbers of total abortions 1972 to 1990 with the number of births to single women 1972 to 1990 we see that abortion on demand has **increased** the numbers of both unplanned pregnancies and births to unwed mothers. Liberals would have us believe that abortion on demand decreases the numbers of problem pregnancies, but clearly this has not happened. Indeed, if the predicted social good resulting from abortion on demand is fewer unwanted children, the opposite has resulted. We may conclude that, by making the consequences of sexual intercourse easier to avoid, legalized abortion has increased the amount of sexual activity among unmarried persons and increased the number of unwanted pregnancies ending in both abortion and live births.

The propensity of liberals and government to exacerbate rather than diminish the social problems to which they turn their attention makes it imperative that conservatives stop these trend lines now through aggressive activism. Otherwise, the trends will accelerate and America will continue to move away from being the envy of the world toward becoming a sociological sewer filled with the malignant discharge of humanity.

The Cultural Waste Dump. American culture is the major symptom of the liberal cancer that infects our national organism. Art stinks. Movies are pornography with good dialogue. Rap music, the anthems of the drive-by shooting, has replaced rock and roll as the corruptor of children. The female culture idol, Madonna, is a bisexual cultural prostitute who sells her soul for the almighty dollar. The homosexual, as a sub-species, is celebrated as something of the "person of the next millennium." Into this cultural waste dump sink our minds, our souls, and our children. A growing fad among teenagers, now, is experimenting with bisexuality, especially among girls. The most popular button on campuses reads "Don't Knock It 'Til You've Tried It," and refers, of course, to homosexuality. In the cultural cliques, you aren't really accepted, anymore, if you haven't had a homosexual affair or two.

Meanwhile, the will of the majority is thwarted at every turn by the liberals who control our culture. School boards

boards force condom distribution onto sixth graders despite nearly violent protests from parents. Even in cases in which 75% to 80% of parents were opposed to teaching the moral, social, and economic benefits of homosexuality, school boards ordered the curricula into the schools. Our Surgeon General says of educating children, "We taught them what to do in the front seat; now it's time to teach them what to do in the back seat."

Leave God and religion and Judeo-Christian ethics out of the conversation for a moment, and look at sexual promiscuity. Does promiscuity solve social problems or cause them? Are historically sexually reserved societies (European) more or less productive than sexually promiscuous societies (South Pacific)? Do sexually active teenagers achieve greater or lesser levels of education, incomes, personal satisfaction than sexually inactive youths? If one answers these questions honestly, one finds that sexual promiscuity, regardless of religious teaching, is a drain both on the society and on the individual.

Religion, once the center of culture, is now a joke to the cultural elite who decide what culture is. Television treats priests, nuns, ministers, rabbis, and devout lay persons as criminals, perverts, and idiots, all for the entertainment of the masses. Smorgasbord Christians, who follow the doctrines they find easy to follow and pass off the difficult ones as "archaic", make a mockery of belief in God. If believing in God and achieving salvation were easy and required no sacrifice, the religion clause of the First Amendment would be unnecessary.

When the Vice President of the United States questioned the wisdom of television producers who exalted the glory of bearing bastard children he was called names by a riled-up cultural elite. The *Washington Post* called his speech "a petty comic performance . . . morally klunky."

Our culture, in fact, is so miserable that one finds it difficult to comprehend. How can a Crucifix in a jar of urine be called art? How can a publicity prostitute like Madonna be called a "shrewd businesswoman?" How can parents tolerate their children learning how to masturbate and make love to a member of the same sex from a teacher? How can we sit in our living rooms and laugh along with evil incarnate as a bumbling priest molests an eight-year-old on the television? Why do we tolerate news programs so filled with glorifications of homosexuality, abortion, and condom distribution that we have to send our children out of the room just so we can learn what the stock market did? WHAT THE HELL HAS HAPPENED TO THIS COUNTRY?

The only good news about American culture is that it can't get any worse, can it?

Conclusion

Things are as bad as I say they are. The America one finds reading Mark Twain or watching a Frank Capra movie cannot even be imagined when viewed from today's perspective. One cannot imagine, for instance, Mark Twain documenting the struggles of homosexual river boat pilots on the Mississippi, or one of his characters trying to procure a package of condoms with which to violate Becky Thatcher. One cannot imagine George Bailey wandering aimlessly and panicked through the streets of Bedford Falls looking for some place to stay after his wife discovered his affair with the paper boy. One cannot imagine Mark Twain willingly paying half of his income in taxes of various kinds -- he complained enough about having to pay less than a quarter. One cannot imagine liberal Democrat Harry S. Truman explaining the proper wearing of a condom to his daughter, Margaret. The ideal of the ruggedly individualistic American is gone completely from reality. Try to picture Europeans leaving their safe and secure homes for America just to escape government meddling and high taxes, as people did in 1815 through 1830 and beyond. Most of the features which distinguished and ennobled American government and American citizens to Alexis de Tocqueville in the 19th century are parcels of history today.

The conservative must contend that Mark Twain's, Frank Capra's, and Alexis de Tocqueville's Americas were the true Americas, and that this country today is a bad imitation. Regardless of personal income and cost of living, our standard of living is currently at an all-time low. We cannot sleep with unlocked doors and opened windows. We cannot walk the streets on warm summer evenings. We cannot honestly answer simple political questions for fear of law suits over racism or sexism. Our children cannot play safely in community parks. Our women are not safe even in their own homes. Our criminals often have living conditions superior to our soldiers' and sailors'. Our heroes are no longer individuals who tenaciously fought their way to the top, but victimized groups who whine and snivel their way into a government program of handouts and handkerchiefs. As compensation for all these freedoms lost, we have fascinating electronic gadgets, inflated salaries, pregnant daughters, gay sons, taxes beyond the conceivable, and a hornet's nest of government social services agencies to help us through the traumas and tragedies of life in modern America -- traumas created by the vary same social services.

Liberalism spares no group its loving, lethal hand of social, economic, and cultural "progress." Blacks who asked only to be judged as individuals have instead been labeled an oppressed group, given quotas, drugs, guns, and poverty. Hispanics who asked only to assimilate have been told not to learn the language of assimilation. To liberals, these results are called compassion, but to the conservative and to the American ideal, these results are called government-sanctioned crimes against humanity. And still, liberals ask for more power with which to segregate more groups into ever-smaller subspecies of human being on which they may apply their expensive, tax payer financed social experiments.

It's time to reassert the American ideal.

The Conservative Creed

Setting down a conservative creed, a set of bedrock conservative beliefs, is always difficult, but has become necessary. Just as necessary is for the conservative warrior to learn, understand, and apply this creed.

In formulating this creed, I have read thousands of pages of conservative text and philosophical dissertations. I am convinced my Conservative Creed accurately states the basic tenets of conservatism and will be useful to the conservative warrior in interpreting the correct position on issues which arise in the future, as well as in interpreting the results of past events.

The Conservative Creed

We believe that governments exist at the will of and to serve the governed.

We believe that a government's only powers are those surrendered to it by those it governs, and that the governed may, at any time, reclaim their powers or deny the government of them.

We believe that the individual is free to do as he wishes within the rules set forth by the majority of his fellow citizens and their elected representatives.

The Conservative Manifesto

We believe that individuals have the right to speak their minds on all political matters.

We believe that individuals have the right to life.

We believe that economic freedom is equal to all other freedoms and the beginning of individual liberty; that government shall not impede economic transactions; and that the power of economic decision resides exclusively with the individual.

We believe that individuals have the right to own personal property and to dispose of that property as they wish.

We believe that identifiable groups have no rights superior to those of the individual, that no group is exempt from the laws deemed right by the majority, and that government may not favor one group before another or before the individual.

We believe that rule of the majority is absolute in all political matters.

We believe that government should not prevent individuals from failing.

We believe that government should not prevent individuals from achieving.

We believe that a government's first responsibility is the protection of its citizens and their property, and that when the government fails to provide such protection, it is the right of the citizens to protect themselves.

We believe that policy decisions should be based on the principle of whether the policy will liberate or bind the individual.

We reject the principle of equality of outcome, but demand equality of opportunity.

We reject the notion of superior rights for certain individuals.

We reject the right of a government to increase its own power without the consent of the governed.

We reject the notion of a right to be free from offensive political speech.

We reject the principle of the perfectibility of man but believe the individual pursuit of perfection paramount to a good society.

We reject the right of a minority faction to thwart the will or overthrow the government of the majority.

We resist the promotion of non-Western cultures as equal.

We resist surrendering individual power to the state.

A common language being crucial to achieving harmony, we reject the idea of government mandated multi-lingualism, but acknowledge the right of individuals to remain ignorant of English.

We acknowledge that education must be promoted and pursued; that government should be neutral toward religions; that individuals have different talents and will achieve according to those talents and the diligence with which they are applied if the individual is left alone; that individuals will fail from time to time despite attempts of governments to prevent it; that our achievements are possible only because of the works of generations which came before us; that we are morally responsible to preserve our freedoms for our posterity; that individuals are morally compelled to assist the advancement of society; that work is morally required of all those who benefit from the society; and that, from time to time, individuals must lend more of their power to the government in order that it may meet the needs of emergencies.

Finally, we believe that the course of history has bestowed upon us unparalleled opportunity and responsibility for the protection, nurturing, and advancement of Western Civilization.

Do not assume that this creed is meant as a substitution for the Constitution of the United States. It is not. It itemizes the common beliefs of conservatives, and, as mentioned before, provides a touchstone for interpreting and forming an opinion on issues.

Living by this creed requires that one resist increases in taxes, bureaucracy, governmental regulation of business, meddling in foreign affairs, granting favored group status to anyone. One cannot abide this creed and consciously vote for a liberal for office, since liberalism must usurp power from the individual to the state in order to achieve its ends. Nor can one abide this creed and demand more government activism, more taxation, or laws which distinguish one group from another based on gender, race, or income.

But there is more to this creed. A creed provides a person with something to affirm, a set beliefs which he can make his own, to which he can point with pride and announce, "These are things I believe." More importantly, by framing these beliefs in the plural, the conservative knows that he is not alone in his beliefs. Even when isolated in the classroom by an intolerant professor and angry students, the conservative will know that others believe in the battle he has engaged, will receive his story of the lonesome fight with approval, and will benefit from his affirming these beliefs. The creed allows conservatives to know that their opinions on issues, if consistent with the creed, will also be consistent with, though not identical to, the opinions of other conservatives from William F. Buckley Jr. to Ronald Reagan. The creed allows the conservative to think originally, rather than relying on the thoughts of others for ammunition when under fire. The creed, if learned and followed, ensures that, while the particulars of the debate may change, the theatre of war may shift, the conservative's beliefs will not, nor will the method of analyzing data and reaching his position change. The creed provides a oneness of purpose for conservatives the way the idea of perfecting society serves liberalism.

This creed is positive in nature, saying what we believe and what accepted truths must guide the functioning of the individual and the society. It provides the individual with a firm and exalted position in his relationship to the government. It does not attack specific policies, philosophies, or religions except to disavow liberal ideas which are inherently dangerous to individual freedom. Again, it is written with increasing the power of the individual in mind.

The soldier in the battle for the soul of America should have an intimate working knowledge of this creed, and should use it when deciding what course of action society ought to take in the face of new crises and opportunities.

Liberal Vs. Conservative Defined

Even with our Creed in hand, we have not solved the problem of being finally able to recognize the difference between liberalism and conservatism in a way that will transcend connotative changes to the words over time.

The term liberal is relatively new to the vocabulary of political philosophy. It was first used to describe the factions in the French Revolution that sought the complete obliteration of the monarchy and all associated institutions. Liberals wanted to execute these changes by executing members of the old system. The term conservative appeared about the same time and was used to describe those who reacted against what they saw as excesses by the liberals. Conservatives, as meant during the French Revolution, were those who desired freedom from the despotic monarchy but wished to retain the basic institutions which existed alongside monarchy. Thus, both liberals and conservatives during the French Revolution desired change, but at different paces and, perhaps, though not definitely, to differing degrees.

Contrary to claims by many political scientists today, liberalism and conservatism maintain essentially the same relationships, both to each other and to the present conditions, as they held during the French Revolution. Modern political scientists tend to define modern conservatism as keeping things as they are, avoiding change, or preferring the status quo. They describe liberalism as seeking to improve society by changing previously accepted norms.

The modern view of liberalism is accurate, but the modern treatment of conservatism is far from exact. Modern conservatism does not *necessarily* seek to keep things as they are. Conservatives believe that, if left alone from undue government interference, *society improves at the fastest pace at which it can safely assimilate that change*. Changes forced upon society by the government will, in the conservative's view, disrupt the equilibrium between what the individual expects and what he receives. In this sense, the conservative believes that *individuals working in their own best interest* will find ways to improve life in a society by putting forth their ideas against the existing ones, allowing a free debate to decide if their proposed change is both good and possible, and living with verdict of the majority.

In a society dominated by conservatives, change will be slow, but constant. More importantly, *changes accepted in the conservative society will almost always work* because the majority will have determined that the proposed change is for the better and that it is workable.

An example of how social behavior improves in the conservative-dominated society is seen in alcohol use among teenagers. Without any significant change in laws effecting the sale of alcohol to minors, the percentage of high school seniors who have used alcohol has been slowly but steadily decreasing since 1987 (National Institute on Drug Abuse, in Bennett). This five year trend is the result of a significant number of teenagers voluntarily not drinking and in a number of adults being less willing to supply teenagers with alcohol. This change in behavior has occurred with little controversy, since there were no new, unwanted laws which forced the change. Additionally, the success of the change is indisputable, since all of the socially destructive statistics associated with alcohol use have improved during this period.

Liberals, on the other hand, tend to believe that society will not improve itself at an acceptably fast pace. *Liberals believe that the state must hold more power than that possessed by the aggregate of its subjects*, that it must attract the best thinkers and specialists in social engineering, and that it must use its power to force upon society changes deemed beneficial and feasible by the elite thinkers in government, regardless of the view of the majority.

In a society dominated by liberals, change tends to be fast paced and frequent. Whether or not the changes are good -- meaning they achieve the intended results without producing offsetting detrimental consequences -- often cannot be measured because there was no prior agreement as to whether the change was needed. Changes in the liberal-dominated society may or may not work, and, because success is not measurable, many people perceive liberals to prefer change for the sake of change. In fairness, liberals try to force changes only if the change will, in their view, benefit the society. But because the success or failure of the changes is judged only by those who forced the changes (the government), virtually all change is perceived by the government as successful.

An example of the liberal method of change is civil rights legislation. Dissatisfied with the rate of assimilation of blacks into the mainstream of society, continuing high rates of poverty and unemployment among blacks, and a frightening level of tolerance for violence and mistreatment of blacks by both whites and some state and local governments, liberals in the 1960s, 1970s, and 1980s jammed through Congress a flood of civil rights legislation designed to force social change on a society which, while largely appalled at the treatment and condition of blacks in America, were not eager for laws that greatly effected the way they behaved, hired, worked, and lived.

The results of the civil rights legislative blitz are mixed, at best. While much progress has been made in the areas of fair hiring practices, equal access to legal redress, voting rights, and equal rights in education, *poverty among blacks has increased, the wage gap between whites and blacks has increased, crime has sky-rocketed* in black neighborhoods, and, after several years of steady decline, race-motivated violence against blacks has been on the increase for four years.

In a conservative-dominated society, much of the progress made in the area of civil rights may still be a dream to many blacks. On the other hand, much of the anti-black backlash and most of the economic depression in black neighborhoods would have been obliterated by now. Indeed, by not forcing change through overzealous legislation, the ammunition that feeds anti-black hate groups today would never have been available to them. This alone would have, at some point in the conservative society, eliminated the most dangerous stereotypes and prejudices held by some whites toward blacks -- small bits of bigotry which might never be completely healed under the liberal system of coerced acceptance. Under conservative dominance, the condition and treatment of blacks in America would have improved, but at a slower pace and with fewer negative consequences.

What conservatives can hope for in a war against liberalism, then, is not a clear-cut victory with liberals raising a white flag and accepting the conservative version of things. More likely, when we achieve victory, it will look very much like the first five years of Ronald Reagan's administration (my concerns about conservative achievements during that period notwithstanding).

When we win, liberals will still believe that government must do ever more. After the victory, liberals will still be around, in fairly large numbers, to criticize our policies, to rally support for their return to power, to advance bizarre theories on improving society (which can be tried only if the majority is forced against its will to accept the experiments). Liberals will continue to seek to empower government by stealing power from the individual. Liberals will continue to gravitate to their usual cliques -- the arts, journalism, academia. Liberals will continue to decry the poor condition of man and the unfairness of capitalism. They will continue to shout for change and more change.

What will have changed, when our victory is achieved, is that something of a balance will have been reached in the liberal enclaves mentioned before. We will have eviscerated the federal government, so that temporary assumptions of power by liberals will have a less drastic affect on the society because the means with which to force their social experiments onto society will first require reassembly. Also, liberal pronouncements will face a sharper challenge, because more people will have been made aware of the stark differences between liberalism and conservatism with regard to their views on the individual's relationship to his government.

> "In this present crisis, government is not the solution to our problem; government *is* the problem."
> -Ronald Reagan, First Inaugural

Conservative Milestones

No discussion of a conservative victory would be complete without at least some examination of specific policy goals which, when achieved, will serve as milestones in our struggle and begin to restore the American ideal. These goals may not be implemented exactly as I describe, but a reasonable facsimile must result from our victory if we are to judge ourselves successful. Failure to achieve at least a majority of these goals in each policy area will mean that our victory is only superficial, like Reagan's, and not complete, as it must be if we are to preserve Western Civilization and the traditional view of America.

Foreign Policy

History has shown that a government cannot devote appropriate attention to its internal problems unless and until its place in the world community is understood and stable. While the conservative tends to be somewhat xenophobic and isolationist, concentrating on internal matters, we must settle our disputes with other sovereign nations before we can turn inward. Additionally, we must avoid the kind of isolationism practiced between World Wars I and II, applying, instead, an aggressive and consistent foreign policy that allows us to a) remain the world's number one military power; b) remain free from involvement in disputes that do not directly affect ourselves, our allies, or our national interests; and c) spend the vast majority of our time concentrating on matters internal to the United States.

Remaining the world's number one military power allows us to dictate the level of our involvement in various international problems. As we found in World War II, when we become a second-rate power others may involve us in wars in which we would not engage if our military strength was such that no one dare challenge us.

Remaining free from involvement in disputes that do not directly effect ourselves, our allies, or our national interest means just that. A free nation cannot morally send its volunteer soldiers and sailors to their deaths if not sending them would not effect the lives of the majority of Americans.

Being able to concentrate on domestic governance, as mentioned before, requires that one not have to spend his time defending the country from outside attackers. Without a firm, consistent foreign policy which is understood by our neighbors (and a military strong enough to enforce that policy), the time that we should spend on domestic governance will have to be spent on foreign problems.

While foreign policy is the most fluid policy area that conservatism must concern itself with, there are certain tenets of conservatism which bear at least indirectly on how we relate to other sovereign nations. Therefore, while I will list firm policy statements, remember that these are overall policy objectives and may have to be altered in the best interests of the country under certain circumstances.

1. The primary purpose of government being the safety of its citizens and their property, the United States will use that amount of force it deems necessary to guarantee its safety.
2. The United States considers the life of each of its citizens more valuable than the lives of any other nation's citizens. When American blood is shed through an aggressive act by or with the consent of a foreign government, the United States reserves the right to retaliate with any and all weapons at our disposal.
3. The United States seeks to be left alone. Therefore, when we are provoked to the point that force is required against a foreign country, the objective of United States' action will be total and unconditional surrender of the enemy. Likewise, the United States will not place its armed forces in harms way unless the objective of our action is total and unconditional surrender of the enemy.
4. Since there is little evidence to defend the United Nations as being anything but a hindrance to the cause of democracy and the advance of American foreign policy, we will withdraw from the United Nations and expel it from our borders.

5. We will maintain our alliances with our Cold War allies only until those alliances become detrimental to our overall foreign policy objectives.
6. We will prevent the spread of totalitarianism in our hemisphere.
7. We will not abide terrorists. Nations sponsoring terrorism against the United States, its citizens, or its allies are subject to our retaliation with any and all weapons at our disposal.
8. Any first use of a nuclear weapon by any country against the United States or its allies will result in the certain and immediate nuclear annihilation of that country.
9. Terrorism conducted within the borders of the United States will result in war against the sponsoring nation with an objective of total and unconditional surrender of the enemy.

Crime

The second aspect of ensuring the safety of its citizens is how a government protects its citizens from each other. Since about 1970, every American administration, state and federal, has failed in this primary purpose.

We are not safe in our own homes, and the danger to our lives and property increases daily. To counter the ever-increasing rate of crime in America, I propose the following:
1. A federal prison will be built in the dessert Southwest capable of housing 20 million prisoners.

2. A Constitutional Amendment will be enacted stating the following:

    a. Upon conviction of a second felony involving a violent crime, the convict will be given his choice of execution or life imprisonment without the possibility of parole.

    b. The right to appeal a sentence of death will be limited to one review at each appellate level superior to the court in which the sentence was delivered. Additionally, appeals will be limited to matters of guilt or innocence only.

    c. Any person serving a life sentence who is convicted of escaping or attempting escape will be executed without further appeal.

    d. The safety of its citizens being the paramount objective of government, when the government is unable to protect its citizens it is the right of the citizens to protect themselves. Therefore, the United States shall not abridge the right of citizens with no personal histories of mental illness or criminal activity from owning, purchasing, or carrying a weapon.

Welfare Reform

Once we are safe from foreign countries and violent criminals, we can devote nearly all our attention to protecting ourselves from our own government. The first area that must be addressed is the welfare system.

While welfare programs in and of themselves are not incompatible with a conservative society, they must meet three critical tests to be acceptable: First, does the program improve the lives of those who participate in it? Second, does the program improve the character of its participants? Third, is the program temporary for its participants?

Obviously, our present welfare system does not meet any of these criteria. Today's programs tend to trap, not only individuals, but succeeding generations in a cycle of poverty and powerlessness. Indeed, it would be very difficult to argue that the lives of participants in our present welfare programs would be any worse if the programs were disbanded tomorrow.

My own inclination is to abolish all federal social programs: social security, Aid to Families with Dependent Children, Head Start, Housing and Urban Development, Food Stamps, Special Supplementary Food Program for Women, Infants, and Children, Low Income Home Energy Assistance, community Planning and Development, Medicare, and Medicaid. But political realities of the present day demand something less than the true American ideal in this area. So, I have set about to describe a welfare system that I believe does meet the tests described above.

1. The Hennessy Family Restoration Program will provide different services for different situations as follows:
    a. Single female (never married) head of household.
    b. Male head of household with or without spouse.
    c. Female head of household; divorced or widowed.

2. Elements:
    a. Housing Voucher: Equal to state's average single family apartment monthly rent redeemable for face value or

less by a landlord or mortgage holder. Vouchers will be based on family size as follows: 1 or 2 adults
    1) and 1 child = 2 bedrooms
    2) and 2-4 children = 3 bedrooms
    3) and 5 or more children = 4 bedrooms.

  b. Free food: Unlimited quantities of beans, peanut butter, milk, bread, and rice through any store upon presentation of UPC scanable identification card. No other food subsidies.

  c. Clothing vouchers: For job application and interviews equal to $300.00 for each adult paid at entry into program. Vouchers may be used only for suit, tie, dress socks, dress shoes, dress shirt for males; or business dress, dress shoes, purse, makeup, pantyhose or stockings for women.

  d. Staples vouchers: Equal to $10.00 per month for each family member which may be used only for:
    1) Soap
    2) Deodorant
    3) Shampoo
    4) Razors
    5) After shave or perfume
    6) Towels and wash clothes
    7) Toilet paper
    8) Tooth paste and brushes

  e. Utilities vouchers: Equal to $30.00 per month plus $15.00 per month for each adult. Cannot be used for long distance phone calls.

  f. School vouchers: See Education below.

  g. Adult education: Adults seeking GED or college degrees evenings or weekends will receive 100% reimbursement for successfully completed courses.

h. Traditional family bonus: $200 per month bonus paid to families consisting of a husband and wife and one or more children. Families headed by a widow or divorced woman receive a $100 bonus.

3. Eligibility:

   a. Single female (never married) head of household is eligible until married or until new pregnancy occurs for a period of two years and while school age children are satisfactorily attending school. Adult must acquire full-time job or combination of jobs equaling 40 hours per week within three months of entering program. Child care is the responsibility of the participant. (The family will become disenrolled and permanently ineligible if the unmarried female head of household becomes pregnant while on the program.)

   b.   Male head of household: Same as 3.a. above, plus one adult must hold full-time job or combination of jobs equaling $40.00 per month. A one-month grace period allowed if job lost due to layoff or business closing only. Children conceived and born while the family is enrolled will not entitle the family any additional benefits.

   c.   Single female (divorced or widowed) head of household: Same as 3.a. above, except job requirement may be waived if divorced spouse is making payments to the family equal to minimum wage multiplied by 40 hours per week.

   d.   Not eligible: Families who have already been on the program a total of two years, unmarried women who became pregnant while previously enrolled, persons with

The Conservative Manifesto

felony convictions, persons who have dependents in more than one household on the program, persons who turn down any job meeting the requirements above.

This program will end the cycle of poverty involved in the present welfare system by providing a lower middle-class lifestyle while forcing participants to seek employment that will remove them from the dole. This program rewards families that stay together instead of rewarding families for breaking up. It provides more than mere sustenance to its participants, allowing them to more quickly get off the dole and into productive labor. It also boots anyone seeking to use this safety net as a hammock. It encourages seeking private assistance providing that private charity may be combined with public programs but may not be used to waive the employment requirements. Finally, it meets the three criteria outlined above for an acceptable welfare program.

Tax Reform

Now that our citizens know what they can expect from government should circumstances demand state assistance, we may turn our attentions to fixing the nation's tax policies once and for all.

The program is very simple, very effective, very efficient. We will eliminate all taxes on investment income, including capital gains. We will eliminate all income tax deductions, credits, and exemptions. We will have only four tax rates:

Household income	Tax Rate
0 to Poverty +10%	0%
Poverty +10% to +400%	8%
Poverty + <400%	10%
Corporations	10%

Since there are no exemptions, deductions, or credits, income taxes for most tax payers will actually go up! Because of the elimination of taxes on investments, however, the total federal tax burden will decrease. Additionally, the Internal Revenue Service will be reduced to a skeleton of what it currently is. Tax preparation will involve a very simple formula: If you made $50,000 and the poverty level for your household size was $10,000, your income was poverty plus more than 400%. Your tax rate is 10% and you owe the government $5,000. The 1040 form will be no larger than a postcard, and all of the instructions will fit on the back.

Under this system, federal revenue would have been higher in 1992 than it was under our present income tax system. Additionally, removing the tax burden from savings and investment will greatly increase the amount of individual and institutional investment in new business and business expansion, creating more and better paying jobs.

Only liberal lies can stop this program from rapid enactment once conservatives gain power.

Social Security

Here is where we break the New Deal's back. Social Security withholdings deplete more money from the private sector than any other single government program. While many individuals cannot be trusted to prepare for retirement, enough can that it is time to sever the dependency-breeding umbilical to Social Security.

1. Individuals above the age of 45 and anyone receiving Social Security benefits at the time Social Security is restructured will retain all benefits and guarantees previously understood.
2. Individuals who have made contributions to Social Security but are younger than 45 on the day of enactment will be given the option of cashing out of Social Security or remaining in the system under the previously understood benefits and guarantees.

3. Individuals who have not begun making Social Security contributions as of the day of enactment will not be entitled to join the program.
4. Persons cashing out of Social Security will be required to invest not less than 90% of their refunded contribution in an approved retirement investment program of their own choosing.
5. All persons not in the Social Security program, including those who cash out, will be required to invest 10% of their monthly gross pay in an approved retirement investment program of their own choosing.
6. All IRA, KEOGH, and 401(k) and other programs qualifying for income tax exemptions under current law will be approved retirement investment programs.
7. Persons cashing out of or not participating in the Social Security program will be entitled to no federal assistance of any kind after the age of 62.

This plan will pay off all those who have contributed to Social Security throughout their lives, give younger workers the option of choosing their own retirement program, and phase out the Social Security Administration completely over time. Billions of dollars will flood into private investments to finance the next big economic expansion. No one loses, except bureaucracy.

Agriculture

Agriculture's romantic place in American history is no excuse for exempting it from the pressures of the market place. Therefore, all federal programs that protect farmers from the economy at large must be dissolved.

While an immediate elimination of farm price support programs may place an undue burden on our economy and food supplies, we must begin disassembling the unsuccessful agricultural programs that have driven farmers into poverty over the past forty years.

Farmers are least prepared for finding a new line of work. As a result, we will have to provide a long lead time, perhaps ten years, to allow farmers who will be forced out of farming by the elimination of federal programs to prepare themselves for employment in different businesses.

The Department of Agriculture, invented by Abraham Lincoln, will return to its original form of being a clearinghouse for information on the latest information on scientific farming. It will get out of the food stamp business with food stamps being replaced by the food voucher system outlined in the welfare reform discussion.

This change will cut government spending by more than $20,000,000,000.00 per year and allow food prices to reach a level consistent with the demands of the market place.

The Balanced Budget Amendment and the Line Item Veto

Two other necessary requirements for the conservative governance of the nation are a Balanced Budget

Amendment to the Constitution and the Line Item Veto for the President.

The best balanced budget amendment will contain the following basic provisions:

1. It will require that expenditures for a fiscal year be equal to or less than the projected revenues for that fiscal year, using as the official revenue projection the median between the Office of Management and Budget's (White House's) projection and the Congressional Budget Office's (Congress's) projection.

2. In time of war or national emergency, expenditures may exceed revenues but only by a vote of two-thirds of all members of both houses of Congress.

3. Increases in income tax rates, corporate tax rates, or the imposition of new taxes will also require a vote of two-thirds of all members of both houses of Congress.

4. If the Congress is unable to achieve a balanced budget by the start of the fiscal year, all federal spending will stop until a budget is approved and signed by the President.

5. All budget surpluses will be applied directly to retiring the national debt. When the national debt is retired, surplus revenues will be returned to the taxpayers directly.

6. Changes to the budget that are revenue and spending neutral once the fiscal year has begun will require a vote by a simple majority of both houses of the Congress.

The line item veto, to be effective, must contain two simple provisions:

1. The President may veto specific items in any spending bill passed by both houses without vetoing the entire bill.

2. Congress may override the President's veto of specific items only by the vote of two-thirds of all members of both houses of Congress on each item vetoed.

Education

Clearly, education is the one area of society which liberalism has completely and inarguably ruined. Our students today leave school with less knowledge than at any time in our history. Illiteracy rates in America are among the highest in the industrialized world. Companies, colleges, and universities are required to devote up to one year preparing each newly hired or matriculated public high school graduate for the task at hand.

The primary cause of our regression in education has been the inordinate attention paid by educators over the last thirty years to the social development of students at the expense of dispensing knowledge. Students today are taught to feel and apologize, but not to think or learn. The liberal notion of relativism contributes to this slide by teaching students, through teachers, that "all things are equal," when, clearly, in the real world, all things are not.

The easiest way to determine what ought to be done to improve education is to find out what the National Education Association, the nation's largest teachers' union, does not want done. Since the thing the NEA is most violently opposed to is vouchers for education, I propose only two changes in education: tuition vouchers and elimination of the Department of Education.

The successful voucher program will have the following features:
1. Each school aged child will receive $1,600 per school year (1993 dollars). This voucher may be used at any school which meets the state's minimum certification requirements.
2. States may not interfere with the curriculum or policies of religious or private schools, except to require that the schools do not discriminate based on race, religion, or national origin. Single sex schools must be left alone.
3. Students who are expelled from the school of their choice because of disciplinary problems will be sent to a reform school run by the state, or a private reform school that holds state certification.

This program will throw competition into education, ensuring that the best schools attract the most students and, therefore, the most money. Bad schools and bad teachers will be forced out of the education business. Bad students will be forced out of the best schools, allowing the serious students to learn. Additionally, the cost of education per student will drop dramatically, allowing more money to be diverted to compensating teachers based on their ability and effort.

Health Care

There is no health care crisis in America, but let's tackle this one, anyway. The problem with health care costs in America stems from the system we use to pay for health care. Private insurance or the federal government, through

Medicare and Medicaid, or both, pay the portion of medical treatment that the patient cannot afford. To keep down costs, insurance companies and the government place arbitrary limits on the prices of various medical services, beyond which the doctor or hospital will not be compensated. This system is bound together by billions of miles of paperwork generated every year, more paperwork in health care than in all other industries combined.

If you want to fix it, you'll have to pass a law banning health insurance plans with deductibles less than, say, $10,000. William F. Buckley Jr. came up with this idea some years ago, and it survives as the only logical solution to the problem. It will force market discipline onto the health care professions which have been exempt for a long time.

Mr. Buckley's system would force patients to seek the best medical treatment they can afford, while providing peace of mind that catastrophic diseases or injuries will cost the patient no more than $10,000. Any other change to the present system (wage and price freezes, mandated coverage, government sponsored universal coverage, etc.) will drive up the cost of medical care while reducing its availability and quality.

Also, bear in mind, that by the American ideal, health care is neither a right nor an entitlement. Making it so distorts its economic value.

Cultural Restoration

The state of American culture is the sum of forty years of liberal dominance in government, media, literature, the arts and entertainment, and, especially, education. We hear many politicians decry the state of society, meaning our culture, but the words are hollow. Government, while largely responsible for our pitiful condition, is almost helpless in improving the culture. This is a confusing state of affairs for Americans, conditioned, as were, to running to Uncle Government to heal all our little wounds. When we come up against a monster which government is unprepared, unwilling, and unfit to fight, we have nowhere, it may seem, to turn.

What government can do to improve culture will result from the policy goals I outlined above. After that, government must get out of our way.

God is a major element of all culture -- with the possible exception of modern America's culture. Lady Margaret Thatcher recently stated our paradox: How can a country whose motto is "In God We Trust" try so hard to remove Him from its national life?

The conservative's first step toward cultural restoration, then, must be very personal: a renewed commitment to the Judeo-Christian tradition.

Second, the conservative must apply traditional moral principles to rearing his children. The next generation is always the most important.

Third, we must fight to restore humanities in our schools. A great Western books course, as much as four or six semester, should be a standard of every college's curriculum. Western Civilization must be a staple of freshman year. High schools and grade schools must drop the vague idea of Social Studies for Western studies. And, of course, we must permit God and His law back into the classrooms if we hope to produce decent citizens.

Fourth, conservatives must make their determination to restore cultural excellence through their economic decisions. What does that mean? Movies, television viewing, and music should be chosen based on our goals for the culture. We must patronize businesses that support our cultural view and shun those that support liberal barbarism.

Finally, we must not be afraid to say that there is right and wrong. We must further this truth by shunning those who do wrong and rewarding those who do right. Without this judgmental approach to life, all hope for cultural restoration is lost.

Summary

The conservative-dominated society will seek to reduce the power of the federal government, eliminate regulations that distort economic realities, and maximize the freedom of the individual to achieve or fail according to his talent and effort.

Since liberals are never satisfied with the pace of improvement in society, they will seek a perpetually more powerful government and increasing government activism. The increased power of government must come directly from diminished power of the individual. Therefore, liberalism will seek to shift power from the individual to the state until all political power has been removed from the individual.

The specific policy goals stated above, if adopted, will serve to indicate a shift in this country from liberal-dominated to conservative-dominated. These policy objectives are consistent with the Conservative Creed, but are not necessarily the only or even the best possible conservative positions. They will prove, however, a clear break from the liberal policies which have dominated our federal government's activities for the past thirty years.

> "Reading maketh a full man; conference a ready man; and writing an exact man."
> -Francis Bacon, *Essays: Of Studies*

Beginning Steps

Now, We Must Arm. No soldier, if given a choice, would charge into battle without ammunition and a weapon. Nor should we charge into what Patrick Buchanan calls "a religious war for the soul of America" without a heavy cache of high explosives. The enemy we fight is lethal and will kill us if we fail to kill it first.

Since this battle will be fought on the plane of thought, the weapons we must arm ourselves with can be conveniently stored in our minds. The delivery system is books. So I've compiled a reading list for the well-armed soldier in the battle.

This list will draw fire from a range of sources. Some will say it is incomplete without Russell Kirk, Adam Smith, Ernest Van Den Haag, and others who formed the basis of conservatism's modern movement. While my list is not complete reading for generals in our war, it is more than sufficient for the foot soldiers who will be my readers. I do not claim that the philosophical treatises on conservatism would be above the ability of the soldiers, but simply that the hand to hand warriors can acquire any additional information they need *during* the battle. My list is must read material *before* the battle.

I should also add that the books on my short list are readily available in libraries, book stores, and book clubs. They represent the spectrum of general information on transcendent issues of which a warrior for the soul of a culture must be able to argue. Thus, I enjoin all of you read these books now:

Democracy in America by Alexis de Tocqueville. Written as a report to the French aristocracy by a French aristocrat visiting America, this book is the base from which flows all understanding of how American democracy should work. Remember, as you read, that Tocqueville visited America only 160 years ago.

Suicide of the West by James Burnham. He starts by observing the advance and retreat of Western Civilization as witnessed by a political map of the world. He parallels the fall of the great age of colonial imperialism with the fall of all things Western brilliantly and inarguably.

The Conscience of a Conservative by Barry Goldwater. This is the book he wrote in 1960, long before he moved back to Arizona and became soft on liberalism. This book comes as close as any to providing a conservative manifesto. It will highlight for you the permanency of our battles with the liberals and demonstrate how quickly we have declined in the last thirty years.

Modern Times by Paul Johnson. This is deep, thick, scholarly history at its best. It traces the key developments in Western culture from World War I (the beginning of "modern times") to the changes away from the modern by Ronald Reagan, Margaret Thatcher, and other conservative nation-leaders of the 1980s. Give yourself some time, a world almanac, and plenty of patience when reading this book. But it is must reading.

Witness by Whittiker Chambers. Chambers is the man who convicted American communism. On the first page he admits his belief that in leaving communism for American Christian capitalism, he was leaving the winning side to join the losing side. You must read *Witness* to know why and how.

Up from Liberalism by William F. Buckley Jr. This is the book that finally called a spade a spade in the battle against liberalism. It is the book that inspired countless conservative causes, including the writing of this manifesto. A conservative who has not read *Up from Liberalism* is like a baseball fanatic who hasn't seen "The Natural."

Parliament of Whores by P. J. O'Rourke. After the heavy reading you completed above, you deserve a break. In Mr. O'Rourke's irreverent and sometimes vulgar diatribe truth peeks out. He gives more ammunition to the opponents of big government than any writer or book on this list, and he's funny while he does it.

An American Life by Ronald Reagan. It's his autobiography. What else can I add?

The Closing of the American Mind by Allen Bloom. The book that scared the hell out of academic liberals in the summer of 1987. After this book, when someone, bewildered, asks, "What the hell's the matter with these kids today?" you'll have an answer.

The Tempting of America: The political seduction of the law by Robert Bork. This book will arm you with ammunition you need to explain why Roe v. Wade was bad law, why our courts are backed up, how to fix the legal system, and what Constitutional law is really all about. It is also fun to read.

Right from the Beginning by Patrick Buchanan. Though this is autobiography of a man who, it can be claimed, has not reached a level of achievement to warrant an autobiography, Mr. Buchanan paints a brilliant, accurate, and detailed picture of what cultural life in American was, can be, and should be. Pat Buchanan's America is the one worth fighting for.

Now, you may wish to subscribe to *National Review, American Spectator, Human Events* or any of the dozens of other conservative journals of opinion. You may want to read Mortimer Adler, Milton Friedman, Russell Kirk, G. K. Chesterton, or Rush Limbaugh. Great! You should. But the books on my list must be read and, preferably, in the order listed.

After completing this reading list, you will be armed. The authors will have provided you the ammunition needed to riddle our liberal foes with intellectual bullets that will land with telling precision and devastating effect. Now, pick up your weapons and march.

Join an Army. Just as no soldier goes into battle unarmed, he doesn't go into battle alone. After you have read the right books, join the right army. This will put you into contact with warriors already in the trenches, men and women who have experienced the horrors of war on the cultural battlefront. Without others, you will not be able to stand the intensity of the battle. Without comrades, you will too easily be drawn to the comfort zone of your television and living room. Without inspired leaders, you will not know in which direction to aim your fire. Join an army.

Our force has many armies, specializing in many different battles of the war. You may want to concentrate your efforts in one area or spread them among many. You may want to work for leadership in your army, or you may be content with fighting the battle. Either way, you need to join with others who think like you, who will provide encouragement and help when your spirit and flesh are weak. Among the groups fighting for the conservative cause are Empower America, the Christian Coalition, the College Republicans, Young America Foundation, the American Conservative Union, the Taxpayers Foundation, The Heritage Foundation, the Free Congress Foundation, Accuracy in Media, Mediawatch, and dozens of others. Any issue of *National Review*, *The American Spectator*, or *Human Events* will lead you to these groups. Find one (or several) that suits your interests and join.

Having identified some quintessential conservative groups, I believe I must devote some space to several organizations which *do not represent conservatism* in any way shape or form, but do *provide ammunition for our enemies* to use against us. Among these groups are the Ku Klux Klan, the Aryan Nation, the Skinheads, and the American Nazi Party.

These groups do not support limited government, they support government activism of the worst kind. They do not promote individual freedom, but group hate. They do not advance freedom, but seek to restrict virtually every aspect of life through terror. They oppose seemingly everything but drunk and stupid. These groups, for the most part, seek to eliminate Blacks, Asians, Mediterraneans, Hispanics, Jews, Catholics, liberals, intellectuals, the wealthy, the poor, libertarians, civil libertarians, agnostics, atheists, Eastern Orthodox Catholics, and, eventually, conservatives, whose bedrock beliefs in the sanctity of life, freedom of expression, freedom of religion, freedom of thought, the free exchange of ideas, and freedom of the individual from government coercion fly in the face of these groups' final solutions.

Conservative armies fight wars for the soul of America through the mind, through enlightenment, by forming and skillfully pronouncing superior ideas in the great debate. The KKK, et al., of course, are incapable of any intellectual discourse, being devoid of a justifiable moral position. They seek not an intellectual victory of ideas, but the physical enslavement of heart, mind, body, and soul. *Conservatives fight against these groups as against other criminals.* Hate groups occupy a moral position equal to

Stalinist Communism and Hitler's Nazism. Let America's contemporary hate groups fear the advancing armies of conservatism as their Nazi ancestors feared the advancing Allies in the spring of 1945.

> "Once to every man and nation comes the moment to decide,
> In the strife of Truth with Falsehood, for the good or evil side."
> -J.R. Lowell, *The Present Crisis*

Fighting The War for The Soul of America

What Next? Bluntly, we must fight. We have learned to recognize liberals and liberalism, we have seen the effects of liberalism, we have concluded that liberalism, in its currently understood meaning, seeks to destroy Western Civilization, and we agree that the suicide of the West is not desirable. So now comes the time to choose sides and fight.

The most important attacks are made at the lowest levels, closest to home. They begin with our children, who must be raised in the traditional Western methods, wherein they develop a strong sense of what a family is, that parents are the loving despots of the home, and that parents are leaders and teachers but not necessarily their best friends. Parents must earn the respect of our children by demonstrating compassion, concern, and guidance, refraining from the modern ideas of boundless experimentation for children. Parents must pay close attention to what their children are being taught in school and in what they are learning from television and playmates. Parents cannot be afraid to tell children that some things are just plain wrong. Parents must be willing to direct children, not just ask them how they feel about something. Parents must understand the obvious: that they are *responsible for the intellectual, spiritual, moral, and physical protection of their children.*

The next battle is also fought close to home: with friends, acquaintances, and co-workers. Too often, conservative opinions are stifled by onerous threats of sexual harassment charges, political correctness violations, and general intolerance of traditional or religious thinking. Conservatives are afraid of these labels and avoid comments that may bring the wrath of the liberal Thought Police. Meanwhile, liberals may say anything, do anything they wish without fear of reprisal. These eight rules should provide ready guidance in your daily battles of the culture war:

1. *Think only of victory.* Any warrior in any war must not consider the possibility of defeat, but, instead, he must envision the final conquest always in his mind, his heart, and his soul. We, too, must keep our victory in mind. I warned against foolish optimism earlier. But confidence in ourselves, because we are right, because we are strong, because we are willing, will give us the strength to pursue this war.

2. *Speak your mind when liberals speak theirs.* We must tell our side of the story every time liberals tell theirs, otherwise we will continue losing by default.

3. *Point out liberal lies, even if doing so causes discomfort or embarrassment.* When someone drops a liberal bumper sticker slogan into a conversation, go ahead and challenge it. If your rejoinder embarrasses the sloganeer, so be it. Liberalism is advanced by repeating lies until they are believed. If you don't challenge these lies at the personal level, we have no hope of overcoming them in the general population.

4. *State the conservative argument even if doing so violates the standards of political correctness.* Political correctness is a liberal euphemism for thought control. Fight it with all your might, as this is the most dangerous expression of liberalism today.

5. *Friends who have fallen prey to liberal lies deserve your bold and assertive assistance.* Just because the person claiming that our taxes are too low is a friend is no reason to let such nonsense go unchecked. A friend, more than anyone, deserves your political honesty.

6. *Affirm conservatism; don't defend it.* If you find yourself constantly defending conservatism ("That's not what I said," "Reagan never said that," "We don't believe in letting people starve," etc.), you are losing the debate. Conservatives must affirm their beliefs in positive statements. ("The 1980s were demonstrably good for America," "Government is not the solution, but the problem," **"Yes, damn it, I AM A CONSERVATIVE!"**)

7. *Prosecute the argument until you have stated the truth, but don't badger your opponent to the point of annoying*

third parties. Generally, once you've challenged the liberal's lie, HE will become irrational. Let him. The goal is not necessarily to change his mind, but win over the individuals looking on. Few people side with someone who becomes irrational as soon as his statements are challenged. But if the liberal does not become irate at your rejoinder, calmly engage him in a strong discourse of the subject using the arguments of the best thinkers of modern conservative thought.

8. *Stop whining*. Don't ask for the government to do a damn thing for you, no matter how important it may seem. The citizens of this country, and the government they have endorsed and ordained, owes you absolutely nothing but to stay the hell out of your way so that you may get to where you want to go. Or so you may at least try.[12] If you start asking the government -- state, local, or federal -- to give you something, you are no better than the rest of the sniveling victims groups out there sucking up tax dollars from the rest of us. What you ought not ask for includes: Social Security, WIC, Food Stamps, better highways, better parks, better playgrounds, a government job, more money for the Small Business Administration, more money for farmers, more money for wetlands protection, more money for the national parks and national forests, more money for education, more money for the elderly, universal health care, more OSHA inspectors, more civil rights laws, more federal laws regarding abortion, more laws regarding anything, more money for anything, more

---

[12] For more discussion of this point, see Appendix.

government for anything. Resist the temptation to call yourself a victim. If you are a victim, it is probably your own damn fault.

Perhaps the most important of these eight tactics of intellectual hand-to-hand combat is *challenging liberal lies*, which we hear everyday. Newspapers, televisions, advertisements, friends, people in line at the grocery store, gas station attendants, spouses, children, and just about any other thing with the ability to communicate may be the source of liberal lies which, we know, become believed if not challenged. The conservative soldier must attack early, hard, and often.

What are these liberal lies? Well, they frequently come in the form of statistics or 'facts', such as:

* There are 6 million homeless people in America. (300,000 is a more accurate number.)

* Hundreds of species become extinct every day. (If this were the case, rats and stray dogs would be endangered species by now.)

* Teenagers will copulate no matter what we do. (Then how does one account for the first 200 years of American adolescent behavior?)

* Homosexuality is involuntary behavior. (Then how can rape be a crime?)

* All women have been sexually harassed at some point in their life. (Then sexual harassment must be involuntary behavior and its perpetrators a protected group.)

* You can't legislate morality. (Then why do have laws against rape, murder, robbery, prostitution, drug use, and monopolies?)

The Conservative Manifesto

The list could go on forever. Another form of liberal lying is in catch phrases, such as:

* The Reagan-Bush years . . . (were, until the 1990 budget deal, the longest period of peacetime economic expansion in our history.)
* The greed of the 80s . . . (Why is seeking to keep the money you earned 'greed'?")
* The right to choose abortion . . . (Where in the Constitution is abortion mentioned as a protected right?)
* The right to a good job . . . (Where in the Constitution is a job guaranteed as a right?)
* The right to a college education . . . (Oh, come on, now.)
* The right to know . . . (Where does the right to know end?)
* The right to health care . . . (Again, consult the Constitution.)
* Tax cuts for the wealthy . . . (increase economic activity, providing more, better jobs, allowing the non-wealthy to become wealthy.)
* Corporate greed . . . (Corporations are fictitious entities, they cannot develop human vices, such as greed.)
* The right to privacy . . . (I thought you said there was a right to know.)

Usually, any sentence that begins with "The right to..." or "We have a right to..." or "It is my right to..." ends as a flat out lie. **Key Point:** If you do not challenge liberal lies, the lies win.

Now we move into the mass movement of conservatism. Taking the battle beyond our doors.

Fight at Work

By now you should understand and appreciate the urgency of the cause and the breadth of the battle field. An area over which liberals seek to exert more and more control is the work place, where unfounded harassment lawsuits and statistics-based hiring and promotion quotas have, in and of themselves, created a hostile working environment for anyone who is not politically correct, liberal, or a member of a preferred minority. Companies succumb to the unfair and often illegal tactics of radical feminist, minority, handicapped, and homosexual rights groups to avoid trouble, rolling over to these groups' ridiculous demands.

In many offices around the country, employees who are permitted to listen to the radio at work may not listen to programs that the Thought Police find objectionable, such as Rush Limbaugh. Not only, then, are liberals limiting freedom of speech of conservatives, they are limiting the conservative's freedom of hearing and freedom of thought.

Many companies require employees to attend sensitivity training sanctioned and facilitated by the most radical Thought Police of the multi-culturalism vanguard elite.

Companies fearing discrimination suits establish hiring and promotion quotas, preventing advancement of heterosexual white males and anyone considered subversive because of his conservative political beliefs.

We must fight fiercely against these encroachments. Do not be intimidated by your company's Thought Police. Demand equal treatment of conservatives by insisting that if Rush Limbaugh is banned then rap music must also be banned. If rap music is still permitted, file a discrimination suit, claiming that the anti-white, anti-woman, anti-authority lyrics create, for you, a hostile work environment. Document, either in writing or on tape, comments made by members of favored minorities that, if reversed, would be considered discriminatory. Challenge unprovable statements made by a facilitator at political correctness training sessions, but avoid disputes over policy unless the policies are based on liberal lies. Do not demand superior rights or preferred treatment. If your company bans Rush Limbaugh because some employees find his show racist (which it is not), you will likely lose the battle to keep him on. But you will win a battle to ban all radio material that you find objectionable, such as rap music or satanic heavy metal. If your employer or fellow employees pose a serious threat to you, wear a voice-activated microcassette recorder at work to establish your innocence.

If your company moves too far to the left in its policies and tactics, enlist the help conservative groups dedicated to preserving the rights of the individual. Even the American Civil Liberties Union chapters in many cities would welcome cases involving denial of your freedom of speech and freedom of listening.

If your company contributes money to causes you find objectionable, find out how much of your compensations go to funding these causes and demand a refund. You won't get it, but you will create a hostile environment for the liberals who made the decision to give profits away. If you belong to a union, remember that you cannot be forced to pay for the political activity of that union. Be on the guard against increases in your union dues, and be vocal in reminding others, especially new employees, that they do not have to pay union dues that support the Democratic National Committee, its candidates, or its friends in political action committees.

Join with other conservatives at your company to buy the company's stock. Two or three hundred employees investing in one stock can have a large say in the board of directors' decisions about policy.

One thing you should do if you work for a liberal or hostile company is to keep resumes and applications out at conservative companies. There is no reason to be loyal to a boss who is disloyal to capitalism.

Stay on the cutting edge of the battle for the soul of America at work. If you bring reading material to work, make sure it is obviously conservative reading material. If you may wear buttons on your clothing, wear conservative buttons. If you dress casually, wear clothing announcing a conservative message. If you have a coffee cup at work, make it a politically incorrect coffee cup.

Fight at Church

If you belong to an organized religion, chances are you have seen your church slide to the left over the past twenty years. Catholics are particularly sensitive to this trend, as are Presbyterians, Methodists, Anglicans, and many

The Conservative Manifesto

Lutherans. Churches must remain conservative if we are to win the battle for the soul of America, and you must fight in these trenches if we are to keep the churches.

Every church has lay committees. Since liberals are, by their nature, more activist than conservatives, these committees tend to reflect, not the make up of the church, but the make up of the National Organization for Women. Joining these committees and encouraging other conservatives to join them will ensure that the committees which guide the activities of our nation's organized religions are hostile to the moral relativity, anti-capitalist views of liberalism. If your church has a steering committee, join it. It determines, to a large degree, what the church's teaching will be. The local congregation's committee selects lay representatives to regional and national conventions which, in recent years, have voted to favor special rights for homosexuals, legalized abortion on demand, and unilateral disarmament. Once again, *if our churches teach liberalism in its most extreme forms, we have little hope for recapturing the great debate in America.*

Fight in the Schools

Education has been a safe haven for radical liberalism longer, perhaps, than any other institution in our society. Recently, conservatives have been winning the battles on school boards all across the country. But much remains to be done.

Leftist education curricula can permanently damage the cause of conservatism, since they will influence the political thinking of entire generations at a time. If schools teach our children that sexual activity is good at any age, that homosexuality is morally equal to heterosexuality, that fathers are not necessary to a family, that Americans are responsible for environmental problems real and imagined, that religion's prohibitions against immoral behavior is the basis for psychological problems of adults, that Western Civilization is the leading cause of social problems, then we stand little chance of convincing our children otherwise. When the school's liberal teachings are reinforced by television programs geared at youngsters and preaching a similar message, we are lost.

The National Education Association is one of the most radical labor unions in America. It funds the pro-abortion organizations, leftist school board candidates, anti-Western think tanks, and a host of other liberal causes. Since time is a major factor in changing the membership of the NEA, we must consider it an enemy in our war and treat it as such. Conservative educators who belong to the NEA must attend its meetings and fight for the elimination of its activities in political areas. Parents must counter the NEA's influence on school boards by organizing parent committees to dominate school board debates. When your board has hearings to determine curriculum policies on such things as sex education, multi-culturalism, environmentalism, and religion, conservatives must attend in legion to ensure fair representation of the conservative position. Be vocal, tenacious, and creative when battling for the minds and hearts of the children.

This battle is one in which we are beginning to turn the tide, but your help is needed now. *Do not let liberals indoctrinate your children.*

Fight in the Streets

Conservatives must begin to stage the mass rallies and marches which have proven so effective for liberals. We need annual parades in every major city and in the nation's capitol to protest abortion on demand, lax treatment of criminals, taxation, government hostility to religion, political correctness and multi-culturalism, and the other major issues of the day. We must organize these protests on a grand scale, ensuring numbers sufficient to draw press coverage, local and national. We must plan events that are creative and disruptive enough to cause a stir. We should seek to offend liberal group-mentality without offending individual rights and freedoms.

Operation Rescue's anti-abortion protests are an example of this type of activism, but Operation Rescue is ineffective because of low turnout and limited range of issues. Conservatives should stage massive rallies to protest liberalism in general. These rallies must draw numbers of people too high for any counter-protest to challenge for attention.

Tax Liberation Day, the day every year when you have earned the portion of your annual salary which is taken in taxes (July 13 this year), should be celebrated with a massive march and rally in Washington, DC, with millions of angry tax payers demanding their money back from the government.

When Congress considers raising taxes, mobs (peaceful, but mobs nonetheless) should fill the Capitol, through which each congressman must pass to reach his seat for the vote. Congress should be flooded with letters and phone calls to such a degree as to prevent the normal operation of the government. These must not be boiler-plate letters, but spontaneous letters from the people. Keeping one's personal freedoms and individualism and economic power intact ought to be enough motivation for these protests. Congressman Bob Dornan and Senator Robert Dole should not have to send out millions of letters in order that Congress receive millions of letters.

Fight Everywhere

There are thousands of other ways to inconvenience liberalism, *gain the attention of the unconcerned, and win the war for the soul of America.* Among these:
- Organize boycotts of everything liberal, and let's start with Ben and Jerry's Ice Cream. Ben and Jerry are a prime example of liberals who got theirs and are now more than happy to support a tax policy that keeps the competition down. Ben and Jerry give 1% of their profits to the Fund for Peace, an organization whose radio commercials, according to William F. Buckley Jr., "all but inspired me to go out and launch a Fund for War." More than just not patronizing disagreeable businesses, boycotts require

The Conservative Manifesto

publicity. You get this by being vocal and creative in your boycott.
- Write letters to the editor of your major daily newspaper. Again, one person's letters, rarely published, will have little effect. But a massive daily delivery of angry, aggressive letters from several hundred conservatives will tip the paper's letters to the editor section in our favor.
- Buy gift subscriptions to major conservative magazines and papers as Christmas and birthday gifts every year. Even if the recipient does not appreciate the gift, if just 100,000 people bought two gift subscriptions every year, our journals of opinion would command disproportionate advertising dollars and gain disproportionate influence in every aspect of American life.
- Campaign for conservative candidates at every level, from the school board to city council, to the United States Congress. To get involved, call your local party headquarters or your state's party headquarters and ask them for the address of your favorite candidate. Do whatever is needed for the candidate once contact is made.
- Run for office when no other conservative will enter the race. But remain true to your conservatism during the campaign. Barry Goldwater did more for the conservative movement in 1964 by carefully affirming his conservative beliefs than he could have done had he moved to the "middle" in an attempt to win. In fact, history shows that conservatives who remain true to their conservative principles fair far better than Republicans who compromise with liberalism. We do not compromise when we are right.

- Shout! Shouting may make you look like an idiot if you do it all the time, but every so often the battle requires a battle cry to get the troops moving. Don't be afraid to raise your voice when the words it carries are the truth and must be heard.
- Stay aware. You must know what liberals are doing if you hope to stop them. Conservative opinion journals and the local paper are the best sources of information on their strategies.
- Keep a sense of humor. George Will offers this advice to conservatives every chance he gets, and he is absolutely right. If you cannot defeat liberalism without losing your sense of humor, you might as well watch the war from the sidelines. P.J. O'Rourke, William F. Buckley Jr., Rush Limbaugh, Robert Bork, Pat Buchanan, George Will, Barry Goldwater, Ronald Reagan, and most other conservative leaders use their senses of humor expertly and with great effect. If you can make someone laugh at a liberal, you've won a battle.
- Exude Enthusiasm. When you need a burst of strength and energy, think of the great conservative leader Jack Kemp, who William F. Buckley Jr. refers to as "America's leading enthusiast." He digresses and rambles and loses his place because he has glimpsed the truth and wants only to share it with the world. That is the attitude that wins.

But no matter how you choose to fight for the American ideal you must *fight for your life as an individual political unit.*

Fight the war for the soul of America as you would fight for your family. This is a key element, since liberalism's most extreme forms will destroy your family. When you

think it better to let a liberal lie go unchecked, remember that the stakes are very high:
- Fight as if someone kidnapped your son or daughter, husband or wife, mother or father. You would fight for all you're worth to get them back. *Liberalism threatens to kidnap the traditional America family.*
- Fight as if a foreign power had invaded American shores, for *what the liberal wants to do to America is as foreign to our heritage as is Soviet Communism.*
- Fight as long as you would to defend your good name, for *liberalism accuses you of racism, sexism, and fascism.*
- Fight as you would against a false accusation in court, for *liberalism seeks to outlaw many of the freedoms to which your American birthright entitles you.*

Don't compromise with liberals

- If you are right, *it is morally imperative to stand by your beliefs*.
- If you were overcharged for a product or service, you wouldn't settle for half the amount due.
- *If your country were overrun by morally depraved, anti-religious, anti-Western invaders*, you would not lay down your arms until the last infidel had been driven from the shore. Now our country is overrun by our own citizens. While we will not compromise the values of life and liberty to get America back, we can and must be willing to fight a long and difficult war for the safety of Western Civilization in the Political, Economic, Social, and Intellectual theatres.

With each passing day our job becomes more difficult. More children have experimented with sex or homosexuality. More condoms, complete with instruction manuals, have been passed out to students. More economic capital has left private hands for the waste dump of Washington. More political power has been usurped from you to some faceless bureaucrat. More of the time of your life has been spent as a slave to the government.

Take up the challenge now. Throw off the chains that bind you to bureaucracy! Bite the hand that feeds you multi-culturalism! Dare to offend that which is offensive! Burn the bridges that lead to collectivism! Reinvigorate the American ideal!

> "God offers to every mind its choice between truth and repose. Make your choice; you cannot have both."
> -Emerson, *Essays: Intellect*

Summary and Conclusions

We have seen that throughout this century, but particularly over the past 40 years, the United States has increasingly transferred political power from the people to the government. This transfer is the bedrock ambition of liberalism, which believes that society does not improve on its own at an acceptably fast pace. Liberalism demands that government take power from the people and use that power to force changes on society through regulation, limitation of freedom, and tax policy which, among other perceived values, redistributes wealth.

We have demonstrated that over the past 40 years, American society has degraded to the point of near collapse. With all its power, government seems unable to protect its citizens and their property from criminal and violent attacks. Moral relativism, a major plank in the liberal platform, has been forced upon society by government and requires that all behaviors -- sodomy, homosexuality, sexual promiscuity -- are equal. Moral relativism has resulted in huge increases in pregnancy among teenagers and unmarried women, increases in the number of abortions, and increases in the number of illegitimate live births. Additionally, moral relativism is the basis for multi-culturalism, political correctness, fanatical environmentalism, attacks on capitalism, and criticism of Western Civilization.

Our economy during this period has grown at a rate one-third of the rate experienced during the first half of this century. We have seen that the liberal solution to economic stagnation is increased taxes, increased regulation, and increased social spending.

But we have also learned about conservatism: what it is, what it is not, and what it can offer the country and Western Civilization. We have adopted a Conservative Creed to ensure that positions adopted by conservatives on various issues are relatively consistent without the need for each conservative to check his opinion with someone else. We have identified several specific reforms of government which will serve both as milestones to demonstrate the real success of the conservative movement (when adopted) and to reverse the transfer of power that has been enriching the government at the expense of the individual for more than 40 years.

We know, now, that conservatives, too, believe in change that improves society, but only if that change results from the voluntary behavior of the majority of the citizens and not from government coercion. Indeed, the conservative believes that government ought to be too small to force unwanted changes on society, as was envisioned by our founders. We have learned that when conservatism reclaims control of the American culture, there will be changes in both our society and our government that will increase the freedoms of the individual and diminish the role of government. With this transfer of power, the individual will incur more personal responsibility than he now holds, but will inherit vastly greater opportunity to achieve, to "pursue happiness" if you will.

Finally, we should have realized that America is in very bad shape -- economically, socially, morally, and culturally. We should understand that liberals still dominate the power centers in America which can effect changes in the balance of power between the individual and the government. We should know that liberalism will not of its own accord surrender power in culture, society, or government, back to the individual, and that, if we are to restore the traditional American ideal of our first 150 years, conservatives must become activist and tenacious. As Abraham Lincoln said, God may provide for those who wait, but what he provides them is what those who worked hard didn't want.

Once again, the American ideal is still with us, in our hearts and souls and minds, if not in our culture, government, or economy. All indications point to our victory once the war begins. Only by standing still can the debilitating fungus of liberal collectivism immobilize the American individual. But right now we are still. We are tranquil, or, at least, we behave as though we are. On our side are strength, truth, and moral certitude. Aligned against us are complacency and the failed old doctrines of a crumbling system called collectivism. We will win if we fight.

The novice, intermediate, or experienced soldier in the war for the soul of America should now be armed and eager for the good fight. This war must now reach its most intense stage. Liberalism must begin to retreat, and conservatism must begin to seize power. Then we must hold that power and fight for more. Finally, once we have returned power to the individual, we must reaffirm Mr. Buckley's assertion in *Up From Liberalism*, quoted in the forward of this book: "I will not cede any more power to the government." Once again, though, we must recapture some power in order to have some not to cede.

Go fight. America is worth the battle.

Appendix

The American Ideal

What is the American ideal? Let us begin this examination by explaining what it is not.

The American ideal is not what Bill Clinton thinks it is. It is not the welfare state. It is not submitting to ever-increasing taxation to fund programs that allow a portion of the population to remain idle. It is not a government that imposes regulations to make life risk free, pain free, or misery free. It is not guaranteed equal results. It is not racial, gender, sexual preference, or handicapped based quotas in everything from hiring to television programming. It is not seeking the safest, most modulated way. It is not a language steeped in euphemisms and apologies. It is not the easy way out.

Nor is the American ideal what Ross Perot thinks it is. It is not government by 1-900 poll. It is not a government imposed austerity program, nor paying more for gasoline, nor equal sacrifice for a non-existent crisis. It is not isolationism run amok.

The American ideal does not fit into any party's platform. It is not realized through huge government programs to benefit some select segment of the economy. It is not realized through expanded small business loans or flood relief bills, student loan programs, tax breaks for favored businesses and industries, agricultural loans, corporate bail-outs, unlimited deposit insurance guarantees, or infra-structure revitalization programs. All these things diminish the importance and independence of the individual.

The American ideal does not manifest itself in multi-cultural orgies or political correctness rallies, both of which divide us into groups rather than empower us as individuals. Hyphenated Americanism is the opposite of the American ideal. As Woodrow Wilson said in 1914, "Some Americans need hyphens in their names because only part of them has come over." The American ideal does not need sensitivity training or new names for old things. The American ideal is not a political unit.

Instead, this American ideal is, at heart, the goal of completely enabling the individual to pursue his dreams without the interference of government. Competition is relished in the American ideal. Score is kept in the American ideal. Results are not equal, only opportunities.

The American ideal has been defined by millions of men and women for more than two hundred years. Thomas Jefferson's speeches and letters were filled with this ideal. Alexis de Tocqueville seemed to understand the American ideal better than his contemporary American, when he wrote:

> As social conditions become more equal, the number of persons increases who, although they are neither rich nor powerful enough to exercise any great influence over their fellows, have nevertheless acquired or retained sufficient education and fortune to satisfy their

own wants. They owe nothing to any man, they expect nothing from any man; they acquire the habit of always considering themselves as standing alone, and they are apt to imagine that their whole destiny is in their own hands.[13]

It is this ideal -- that I am responsible for myself, my own actions, my own mistakes, my own successes -- that is the American ideal.
Ronald Reagan, in his acceptance speech at the 1984 Republican National Convention, clarified and augmented this ideal:

We celebrate the right of each individual to be recognized as unique, possessed of dignity and the sacred right to life, liberty, and the pursuit of happiness. At the same time, with our independence goes a generosity of spirit more evident here than in almost any other part of the world. Recognizing the equality of all men and women, we're willing and able to lift the weak, cradle those who hurt, and nurture the bonds that tie us together as one nation under God.[14]

Here we must clarify the contrast between our belief in the sovereignty of the individual and the equality of all men and women. During this century, the idea of equality has

---

[13] Alexis de Tocqueville, <u>Democracy in America</u> (1984, New York: Mentor Books) Richard D. Heffner, ed.

[14] Ronald W. Reagan, <u>Speaking My Mind: Selected Speeches</u> (1989, New York: Simon and Schuster).

become distorted by socialist and communist ideas of total equality; i.e., equality of outcome. While one may wish for a world in which each person died with the exact same net worth as every other person, nothing in all of recorded history, science, anthropology, sociology, philosophy, or religion tells us that such equality of outcome is possible or that its pursuit is desirable. In fact, history does seem to prove that experimentation with equality of outcome fails miserably, leaving the vast majority of souls living under these experiments trapped in a lifetime of slavery to an omnipotent collectivist state.

Tocqueville carefully itemized the idea of equality that was accepted and understood prior to this century: "Equal rights may exist of indulging in the same pleasures, of entering the same professions, of frequenting the same places; in a word, of living in the same manner and *seeking wealth by the same means.*"[15] Clearly, then, in Tocqueville's time, equal was not understood as equal possessions or equal outcomes, but *equality of station* -- the idea that no man was the metaphysical inferior or subservient of any other man.

Equality is achieved, in the material sense, only at the expense of liberty. The individual must allow some third party to determine what his worth is, and either augment his holdings with property taken from others, or confiscate some of his property to augment that of another.

Tocqueville's and Reagan's equality requires no such third party (government) action. In the founder's

---

[15] ibid.

understanding of equality, all individuals are equal in the eyes of Gods, but also in their right to *pursue happiness*. If his pursuit is weak, misguided, or indecisive, if nature has endowed him with few natural talents, if Providence should divert him from this pursuit, or if anything hinders his pursuit, he at least had the opportunity, like all others, to try. Jefferson believed in a natural aristocracy among men based on talent. Tocqueville, too, hinted at the inevitability of diverse results when said of the American individual: he owes nothing to anyone and is owed nothing by anyone.[16]

In the American ideal, the individual must decide what to pursue, how to pursue it, and the criteria by which he will judge his success or failure in that pursuit. He knows at the start that there are no guarantees, that competition will be tight, that in failing he could lose everything. But he pursues to his hearts content. He knows the risks that are knowable and knows that some risks are unknowable. He knows that most men do not achieve either wealth or happiness, only parts of them, and that the odds are stacked against him. He expects no help in his pursuit nor compensation for losses should he fail. He understands that the greatest risks bring the potential for greatest achievement and determines for himself how much risk to which he will expose himself. He does not expect government to take his neighbor's farm or car or money to even things out should disease or famine or flood destroy his property or his ability to pursue happiness.

---

[16] ibid.

The American ideal is, simply stated: first comes the individual: everything else is overhead.

Bibliography

Bennett, William J., (1993), *The Index of Leading Cultural Indicators*, Washington: Empower America, The Heritage Foundation, Free Congress Foundation.

Bloom, Allen, (1987), *The Closing of the American Mind*, New York: Simon & Schuster.

Bork, Robert H. (1990), *The Tempting of America: The Political Seduction of the Law*, New York: The Free Press.

Buchanan, Patrick J., (1988), *Right from the Beginning*, Boston: Little, Brown, and Company.

Buckley, William F. Jr., (1959), *Up From Liberalism*, Briarcliff Manor: New York, Stein & Day first paperback edition, 1985.

Burnham, James, (1985, 1986), *Suicide of the West*, Lake Bluff, Illinois: Regnery Books.

Chambers, Whittikar, (1952), *Witness*, Washington: Regnary Gateway. Copyright renewed 1980 by Esther Chambers.

Goldwater, Barry, (1960), *The Conscience of a Conservative*, New York: Victor Publishing Co.

Goldwater, Barry, with Jack Casserly (1988), *Goldwater*, New York: St. Martin's Press.

Johnson, Paul, (1991), *The Birth of the Modern*, New York: HarperCollins Publishers.

Johnson, Paul, (1983), *Modern Times: The World from the Twenties to the Eighties*, New York: HarperCollins Publishers. Previously published in England under the title *A History of the Modern World: From 1917 to the 1980s*.

Murray, Charles, (1984), *Losing Ground: American Social Policy 1950-1980*, New York: Basic Books.

Murray, Charles, (1988), *In Pursuit of Happiness and Good Government*, New York: Simon and Schuster.

O'Rourke, P. J., (1991), *Parliament of Whores: A Lone Humorist Attempts to Explain the Entire U.S. Government*, New York: The Atlantic Monthly Press.

Reagan, Ronald W. (1989), *Speaking My Mind: Selected Speeches*, New York: Simon & Schuster.

Reagan, Ronald W. (1990), *An American Life: The Autobiography*, New York: Simon & Schuster.

Tocqueville, Alexis de, (1984) *Democracy in America*, New York: Mentor Books; Richard D. Heffner, ed.

Weise, Elizabeth, (1993), "Author believes America is now a nation of whiners, 'victims,'" Associated Press, in *The Day of New London*.